NORTHERN LIGHTS

ONE WOMAN, TWO TEAMS, AND THE FOOTBALL FIELD

THAT CHANGED THEIR LIVES

CATHY PARKER

WITH **DAVID THOMAS**

W PUBLISHING GROUP

AN IMPRINT OF THOMAS NELSON

Published in Nashville, Tennessee, by W Publishing, an imprint of Thomas Nelson.

Thomas Nelson titles may be purchased in bulk for educational, business, fund-raising, or sales promotional use. For information, please e-mail SpecialMarkets@ThomasNelson.com.

Scripture quotations are taken from the Holy Bible, New International Version®, NIV®. Copyright © 1973, 1978, 1984, 2011 by Biblica, Inc.® Used by permission of Zondervan. All rights reserved worldwide. www.Zondervan.com. The "NIV" and "New International Version" are trademarks registered in the United States Patent and Trademark Office by Biblica, Inc.®

Photos in the insert are courtesy of Terry Brown, Budd Goodyear, and Diane Larson Photography. Used with permission.

Any Internet addresses, phone numbers, or company or product information printed in this book are offered as a resource and are not intended in any way to be or to imply an endorsement by Thomas Nelson, nor does Thomas Nelson vouch for the existence, content, or services of these sites, phone numbers, companies, or products beyond the life of this book.

ISBN 978-0-7852-2381-8 (eBook)

Library of Congress Control Number: 2019901087

ISBN 978-0-7852-2380-1

Printed in the United States of America

19 20 21 22 23 LSC 10 9 8 7 6 5 4 3 2 1

PRAISE FOR
NORTHERN LIGHTS

"I was recruiting the Parkers' son, Kyle, during the time Cathy was spearheading the efforts to put an artificial football field in Barrow, Alaska. It is a miraculous story that should be told."

> —Dabo Swinney, Head Football
> Coach, Clemson University

"I count it a privilege to recommend to you my friend Cathy Parker. Cathy has a heart to encourage young athletes and their families, and she knows firsthand the numerous challenges they face. I refer to her incredible story as a 'God story,' one that is impossible apart from the power of God."

> —Pam Tebow, Mother of Tim Tebow

"I am delighted to see how God has used Cathy Parker, my dear friend, to persevere through an otherwise seemingly ridiculous and impossible task. Why would a woman who lives in Florida ever push through so many limits and obstacles to spearhead building a football field for a remote and desolate place in Alaska—a place she never been and for people she had never met—just from watching a television documentary? Because that's Cathy.

"I am extremely excited and proud of my friend for her continued drive to push the envelope and expand her horizons to bless others. I wish her continued success and blessings as she continues to be inspired and led by the Holy Spirit—he is our guide and comforter."

> —Tammy Wilson, Mother of Russel Wilson

"It's truly a heart-warming story and one that will appeal to a large audience. I very much admire how you have stayed with this project through difficult times when many would have given up."

> —Wayne Weaver, Former NFL Team
> Owner of the Jacksonville Jaguars

"Cathy, you are indeed an inspiration to us all. We followed with great interest your fund-raising efforts to provide a field for football players thousands of miles from your home. At first, I wondered what your motivation could be. The more I read, the more I saw that you were nothing but a Football Mom, a mother concerned about where kids play their sports and ensuring that they have opportunities in sports. As a fellow Soccer Mom, I relate to your motivation and commitment to kids.

On behalf of the kids of Barrow and Alaskans everywhere—a big Alaskan thank you!"

—Lisa Murkowski, United States Senator, Alaska

NORTHERN LIGHTS

. . . so that people may see and know, may consider and understand, that the hand of the Lord *has done this . . .*

—Isaiah 41:20

CONTENTS

Chapter 1: A Higher Calling | 1

Chapter 2: "It's You" | 9

Chapter 3: Resenting Football | 13

Chapter 4: Season of Change | 21

Chapter 5: Men Built for Others | 29

Chapter 6: Introduction to Barrow | 41

Chapter 7: Obedience Plus Inspiration | 49

Chapter 8: It's Official: Project Alaska | 57

Chapter 9: "He'll Prepare Their Hearts" | 67

Chapter 10: A Family in the Media | 75

Chapter 11: Unexpected Help | 85

Chapter 12: A $40,000 Miracle | 95

Chapter 13: Welcome to Jacksonville | 105

Chapter 14: Fun in the Sun | 113

Chapter 15: A Life-Changing Week | 119

Chapter 16: Critical State | 131

Chapter 17: Black Monday | 143

CONTENTS

Chapter 18: Warm Reception | 149

Chapter 19: Friday Night Sunlight | 161

Chapter 20: One More Miracle? | 171

Chapter 21: Closing the Books | 179

Chapter 22: No Desire for Normal | 185

Chapter 23: A New Barrow | 195

Appendix 1: 2007 Barrow Whalers Roster | 203

Appendix 2: 2007 Bartram Trail Bears Varsity Roster | 207

Acknowledgments | 211

About the Authors | 213

CHAPTER 1

A HIGHER CALLING

Barrow, Alaska. You can't go farther north and say you're in the United States. It's closer to the North Pole than to Seattle, Washington—by almost seven hundred miles.

Temperatures in Barrow rise above the freezing mark about 120 days per year. During the coldest months, they can dip into the minus-fifties, with wind chills of more than 70 below. The town of more than four thousand people sits on permafrost as deep as thirteen hundred feet, making it impossible to grow grass and trees. That permanently frozen ground prevents the building of roads to connect Barrow to the rest of Alaska, so you can only get there by air or by sea. Barges can make their way into Barrow only during the two summer months, when the ice packs move out into the Arctic Ocean.

Barrow is the last place on earth you would expect to . . . well, there are a lot of ways to finish that sentence. Until 2007, "see a bright blue and yellow football field" was one of them.

I first heard of Barrow on a Sunday morning in October 2006, when the town interrupted our family's weekly pre-church routine. Our four children had changed into casual clothes for church and were watching ESPN. I was in the kitchen, making a batch of homemade blueberry muffins and chatting with my husband, Carl, as he sat at the kitchen table. Sunday mornings in our home were relaxed, by design. We wouldn't leave for church until about ten thirty, and Sunday was our one day of the week when we didn't have to rush in the mornings to get somewhere.

I was preparing to slide the muffins into the oven when our oldest, Kyle, called out to us: "Mom, Dad! You've got to come in here and see this!"

I shoved the muffins into the oven, and Carl and I hurried into the adjoining family room. Kyle quickly caught us up on a story about the Barrow Whalers, a high school football team north of the Arctic Circle, in far north Alaska, playing their first season.

Carl sat in our oversized chair. I took a spot on the ottoman in front of the chair and leaned back against his knees.

The reporter asked how many of the players had not played football before joining the team. It looked like almost all, if not all, raised their hands. The story drew us in because of the school's 50 percent dropout rate. The Barrow youth had high rates of depression and suicide too. Drugs, alcohol, and the extreme climate contributed to the problem. High school and community leaders seemed desperate to find a solution, especially after two youth murdered a taxi driver in a robbery that netted $100 to buy drugs. They surveyed students to ask what would help them engage more in school. The students' number-one answer was surprising: a football team.

Tears welled up in my eyes as I thought about the social problems these young men were facing. Yet what really caused my stomach to tighten was seeing the Barrow Whalers' field. In the absence of grass, the field was an unsightly mix of packed dirt, mud, and gravel. The players displayed the cuts and bruises they had received from its rocky surface.

Our football-playing sons cringed.

Ruts in the field caused by melted permafrost led to sprained ankles. Without grass, lines could not be painted onto the field. Instead, the field was lined with flour, which provided a welcomed postgame meal for the resident birds.

Sitting in the comfort of our home in Jacksonville, Florida, with our subtropical climate and lush, green sports fields for our children to practice and play on, my heart broke considering the physical sacrifices those kids were making to play football. To play a game my family had been born playing.

I turned to see tears in Carl's eyes too. He was a high school coach who had played in the National Football League. Carl could relate to the players as well as the coaches' plight in starting a program in such adverse conditions.

ESPN reporter Wayne Drehs did a great job of presenting both sides of the controversy in Barrow over adding football. As much as my family loved sports, I could sympathize with the teachers there who cited other needs that could have used the funding and complained that football benefited only a certain part of the population. Yet, I also knew the unifying power of sports. Sure, Carl and I had witnessed what can be the damaging side of sports, but we'd also seen how sports can reach across a range of socioeconomic groups, bring the youth together into a team, and develop young men to become difference makers in society.

The story moved me emotionally. As it ended, I had no idea that it would move me to action.

Taking the time to watch the story forced Carl and me into rush mode to get ready for church. We swiftly changed clothes in our bedroom as we discussed the story.

"I understand the educators' points about needing books, computers, and laptops," I told him. "But what good are they if the kids are not going to school? What good are they if the kids are ending up in jail? Or committing suicide?"

"I know," Carl said.

"You know," I continued, "that football program is going to save the lives of those young men."

"Yeah," he said, "you're right."

A SPORTS FAMILY

ESPN and blueberry muffins.

The morning the Barrow story aired wouldn't have been an official Sunday morning in the Parker household without our four children—ranging in age from twelve to seventeen—getting their ESPN fix while I made muffins from scratch.

The muffin recipe came from my momma. The ESPN-watching came from Carl.

My husband played six seasons of professional football, including two in the National Football League. Kyle, Collin, and Kendal grew up throwing, catching, hitting, and kicking balls. When our daughter, Cara, came along, we hoped she would lead us into the land of music and dance recitals. But the boys insisted on putting a football helmet on her head and a ball in her hands, and as soon as Cara was old enough to express her athletic aspirations, our hopes were dashed.

We were a sports family through and through. Mix in witnessing in our home each week the positive impact football could have on teenage boys, and we were ripe to be pulled into a moving sports story.

During Carl's two seasons coaching high school football, we had been hosting players at our home on Thursday nights. We'd rotate groups of players by position, with anywhere from twelve to eighteen eating dinner with us each week during the season. It was a challenge satisfying the appetites of that many high school football players, so every week I prepared meatball subs on French bread with salads, followed by homemade banana pudding for dessert. One player ate so much that Cara often came home from softball practice to find no food left for her.

The players came to count on the Thursday dinners in our home, and we relished the opportunity for them to see Carl in a role outside of their coach. That included being a dad to his sons and daughter and a father figure to their teammates, some of whom didn't have a dad at home.

As I had watched the ESPN story, I'd wondered: *If football could make a noticeable impact in a comfortable, affluent area like ours, how many lives could it change in Barrow?*

My conversation with Carl about the Barrow story ended before we left for church, but the needs of those players and the condition of that field didn't leave my mind.

RECEIVING THE ASSIGNMENT

We attended a start-up church of about fifty people meeting in an elementary school. The six of us took up an entire row of seats. The pastor, Ron Morris, and his wife, Susan, often made up half of the worship team, with Pastor Ron playing drums. The Morrises had five children. Our two families accounted for almost a quarter of the attendees.

During worship that morning, my mind drifted back to the ESPN story. I kept thinking about what it would be like to see that pitiful field transformed into a green, artificial turf field, eliminating the cuts and bruises the players now suffered from the rocks. Ron was a good preacher, but I can't recall one point from his message that morning. Or his topic. I'm usually a notetaker during sermons, but that morning I took no notes.

Whatever Ron said must have carried a tone of encouragement, though, because as he preached, I progressed from being moved by the story of the Barrow players to sensing that God was placing it on my heart to somehow help them.

Our sons played on a wonderful grass field at Bartram Trail High School. Jacksonville had hosted Super Bowl XXXIX in 2005, and the NFL chose Bartram Trail as the practice facility for the New England Patriots. The school already had one of the best high school fields in Florida, but NFL and turf guru George Toma—his nickname was "the god of sod" because of his magic with grass fields—built a new practice field for Bartram and upgraded the game field to professional standards. Our sons played and practiced on fields of the quality that professional and top-level college teams were accustomed to.

Also, Carl held two jobs at the time: offensive coordinator for Bartram Trail's football team and assistant director of Parks & Recreation for St. Johns County. As part of his Parks & Rec job, Carl was overseeing the installation of artificial turf fields to replace the overused grass fields. Our community was growing so rapidly that the county couldn't keep its fields properly maintained, and Carl had researched turf fields and compiled an eighty-page binder of information to present his case to the county for installing the fields. From talking with Carl and reading through his binder, I knew a bit about the cost and benefits of replacing grass fields.

If we need artificial turf fields here, I thought as Pastor Ron preached, *how much more do they need one in Barrow? They can't even grow grass. How much more do they need it than we do?*

Right there, in the middle of the sermon, I realized there was something we could do for the team in Barrow—give them a turf field.

Immediately, my thoughts shifted to how we could make that happen—how we could pay for a field in Barrow. I had sales training and experience selling a variety of products. My sales knowledge kicked into gear.

Okay. We'll present this to some sports company, like Under Armour or Nike, that can pay for it. It will be costly, but the story is so compelling that certainly there will be sports companies that will want to be part of providing a field for Barrow. I'll have to put together visuals and a compelling case for support. But I can do that. I can get them to write a check. This will be fairly simple.

Then my thoughts turned to the Barrow coaches. Based on the ESPN story, I assumed they needed a lot of help with football X's and O's, because almost all their players had no experience playing football. I believed our school's coaches could train Barrow's coaches.

I've had many ideas during my life that I didn't see through to completion or that didn't work out for a variety of reasons. But this one was different. It was more like a vision than an idea, because I could see those same young men from my TV screen playing on a turf field. I could see their uniforms untorn, their skin uncut because of gravel in their field.

I wanted church to end immediately (sorry, Pastor Ron) so I could tell my family about what I believed God wanted me to do. But before we left after the service, because we met in a school, all the families had to pitch in on the teardown, stacking chairs and taking down the portable sound equipment.

By the time we finished and got to our Chevy Trailblazer, I was so eager to tell my family the news that before I closed my passenger-side door, I turned to my kids, who were climbing into the back two rows, and said, "I have an announcement to make. God showed me something. We're going to raise some money, and we're going to give that team in Alaska an artificial turf field like ours. We're going to teach them how to play football."

Everything I knew about Barrow, Alaska, had come from about ten minutes of an ESPN story. But I knew that God had given me an assignment.

My first steps were born not out of inspiration, but out of obedience.

CHAPTER 2

"IT'S YOU"

Based on my kids' reaction to my big announcement, I quickly identified my first obstacle in putting a football field in Barrow: gaining my family's support. Accustomed to their mother coming up with crazy ideas, all the kids laughed except Cara. (To this day, she reminds me she was the only one of the four who initially thought I had a great idea.)

"Mom, that's impossible," Kyle said. "There are no roads going to that place."

That wasn't the reaction I expected. Kyle had been the one who'd called for Carl and me to come watch the story, so I thought the idea would at least excite him.

FIRST STEP

At home, I restarted the field conversation with Carl, asking if he could set up a meeting for me with the turf company representative he'd been dealing with for the county's fields.

"They are not going to want to put a field in Alaska," Carl said.

"Well, you don't know," I argued. "Let's just talk to him about it."

I bugged Carl for three days until he finally relented.

"Okay," Carl agreed at last. "I'll get us a meeting with him."

About a week later, Carl introduced me to Steve Coleman, a regional director for ProGrass. Finally, I could take the first step.

I am entrepreneurial by nature; Carl is the practical type. Opposites attract. He used to ask why I always thought of crazy stuff to try. I found the answer when our church was working through the *40 Days of Purpose* study guide. Following one late-night discussion when Carl had failed to see my brilliance in always coming up with great ideas, I awoke at three o'clock in the morning still upset over our disagreement. Carl was correct. I believed there was something wrong with me. I always seemed to have thoughts that were much bigger than other people's. I picked up my book and started reading the next day's material, which happened to describe people who possess an entrepreneurial spirit. *That's me!* I thought. Then I woke up Carl so I could explain to him why I am the way I am—God made me that way.

Although I am a risk-taker, I tend to envision the finished product much easier than I imagine the process of getting there. Our pastor once described me as someone who fires, then aims, and *then* gets ready. I reluctantly admit that's accurate.

Realizing that God made me a visionary had given me the freedom to step out with confidence when I had an idea. Little did I know that what I'd read in *40 Days of Purpose* would have such an impact on me. I truly believed that I was wired differently, that I had vision.

Meeting with the turf company representative would serve as my first real test, because Steve would be the first person to hear my idea who could fit into my plan for putting a field in Barrow. I walked Steve through a summary of the ESPN story and my desire to give the Whalers a field.

"Oh, man," he said. "That's a great idea. I think the people who own the company, they'll be all over this. They're very giving."

I looked at Carl and grinned.

Steve, Carl, and I tried to estimate what installing a field in Barrow would cost. We knew nothing about transportation needs for all the field-related products, but we came up with a figure of $500,000. Although that would prove to be significantly short of the final total, I left considering that meeting a win because the turf company was on board.

I had not yet attempted to contact anyone in Barrow, because I first wanted to get a realistic idea of what would be required to give them a field. But on my way home from that meeting, I told myself, *This is actually starting to come together.*

A GOD-SIZED TASK

I'd been talking about the field with close friends, and they had been encouraging me. I was excited about the idea, but the more I learned about what building a field in Barrow would entail, the more I realized the enormity of the task I was undertaking. ProGrass's involvement increased my nervousness. I believed I had a good idea, which Steve confirmed, but I had been hoping that someone more qualified would show up and take over. Either would provide my exit ramp off the project.

The more I researched Barrow—its harsh conditions and its isolation—the more enormous the project became. I had never attempted anything like this. I started to doubt I could pull it off.

I am the youngest of six children. I talked about the idea every day with two of my sisters and my oldest brother. During a phone call with Mary Ann, who is six years older and the closest to my age, she asked how the field was progressing.

"You know, I got to thinking about that," I told her. "I'm sure somebody saw that story—perhaps a current NFL player or someone who has a lot of money. I'm sure somebody saw that who has a lot more influence, a lot more connections, and a lot more resources than I do."

Mary Ann got quiet. She tends to do that when she's thinking of the best possible response. Wisdom usually follows her silence.

"No, Cathy," she told me. "God gave *you* that vision. You're the one that's got to do it. It's not somebody else doing this. It's you."

Doggit!

I knew Mary Ann was correct. It *was* my assignment.

I had no idea of the journey ahead, or the miracles I would experience along the way. Just like I hadn't known that the miracle that saved my family, that removed the deep-seated resentment I held toward sports, would position me to steadfastly believe that football could unify a community and change the lives of young men seemingly a world away.

CHAPTER 3

RESENTING FOOTBALL

From the moment I met Carl and we became friends in junior high, I knew he loved football. As our relationship grew into something more over the years, until we were finally dating during our senior year of high school, so did his abilities as a wide receiver. Carl landed several scholarship offers and chose to attend Vanderbilt University in Nashville, Tennessee. Having a front-row seat to see Carl fulfill his dream of playing college football thrilled me, even as I stayed home to attend what was then Valdosta State College.

Our freshman year, Carl and I spent most of our money on late-night, long-distance phone calls. During the spring semester, a couple in Nashville felt sorry for Carl and loaned him a car so he could drive home to see me.

"I'm not going back to school without you," he told me.

We devised a plan to be together for the next school year. I had been working part-time at a shoe store and putting aside what I didn't spend on phone bills. I applied to Belmont College, which was less than a mile from Vanderbilt's campus.

Carl and I married on July 20, 1984. We both were nineteen and ready for married life! Or so we thought.

While he headed off to Nashville for training camp, I stayed in Valdosta with plans to complete my summer internship and then join him before the fall semester. Those plans changed a few weeks after the wedding when I received a call informing me that Carl had suffered a serious knee injury during a practice. There was concern the injury could end his football career. I headed immediately to Nashville to be with him.

Carl's surgery to repair the torn ligaments went well, and although the doctors told him he would be able to play football again, they ruled him out for the upcoming season. That news devastated Carl, especially after he had played sparingly as a freshman. The honeymooners' bliss made it easy for me to care for Carl as his knee recovered, but I felt helpless to deal with the near depression Carl experienced over being unable to play.

I had my own course load at Belmont to manage, and the reality of my schedule and our tight finances was already starting to set in. I needed to get a job on top of caring for Carl and going to school, and I found full-time work in sales. I worked hard to keep up with my classes and stayed frugal with our money. Carl was one of two married players on the team, and because we lived off campus, we were basically on our own for food. I recall one morning when our breakfast was hot dog buns without the hot dogs. We couldn't even afford to butter the buns. Another time, we ate hot dogs without the buns.

That first year of marriage was difficult. We made it because all we had was each other and a hope rooted in what could be ahead for us. I believed the sacrifices we were making and the financial struggles would be worth it after Carl earned a degree from a great university like Vanderbilt.

Carl recovered completely from the knee injury and shined on the football field for the rest of his college career, positioning him to be drafted in the NFL's 1988 draft. A Vanderbilt degree *and* a career in the NFL were far greater rewards than we could have imagined.

TURNING PRO

The draft day scene was much quieter for Carl than it is nowadays. We were alone in our apartment for what was then a two-day draft, expecting him to be selected but unsure of which round. The Cincinnati Bengals ultimately drafted Carl on the second day, in the twelfth and final round. We celebrated like a couple of giddy kids! Yet with the move from Nashville to Cincinnati, everything about our lives changed.

We were even farther from our families, plus we had left behind our friends at Vanderbilt. As a rookie taken in the final round, Carl wasn't making big bucks by NFL standards, but it was a ton of money compared to what I made as a working student in Nashville. For the first time as a couple, we had money to spend.

The Bengals won their first six games of Carl's rookie season on their way to qualifying for the postseason with a 12–4 record. Carl's teams at Vanderbilt had not been successful. For both of us, winning was fun!

Carl's wildest dreams came true when the Bengals beat the Buffalo Bills in the AFC Championship Game to advance to Super Bowl XXIII. Although the score didn't turn out as we'd hoped—the Bengals lost 20–16 to the San Francisco 49ers—Carl still got to play in a Super Bowl in his first season in the NFL. There are many players who go through an entire career without reaching the Super Bowl.

To make that year even better, we learned that I was pregnant!

Even with the excitement from the team's success and the pending arrival of our first child, the money Carl made kept us from recognizing the toll that his joining the NFL was taking on our relationship. In Nashville, despite all the material possessions that we didn't have, the most valuable thing we did have was each other. In Cincinnati, though, Carl took full advantage of the pro football lifestyle. He went out to bars with his teammates, many of whom were single. Plus, the team played half of its games on the road, and that meant travel. And travel meant more going out to bars to avoid the boredom of hotel rooms. Carl placed himself in situations that he had not previously.

The foundation of our marriage was each other, and that foundation seemed to be crumbling.

It was Carl's strong faith that had first attracted me to him. Now, he rarely spent time with me. I knew our marriage was in trouble, but I had no idea just how rocky it would become.

Carl played primarily on special teams as a rookie and he worked hard during the offseason and at training camp to keep a roster spot for his second season. Things were looking promising on and off the field, but two weeks after Kyle was born, we experienced the harsh business side of the NFL. The Bengals had won four of their first five games, but key players were suffering injuries. In what was a fairly common practice at the time, one of the coaches from the Bengals asked Carl to fake an injury so they could place him on the injured reserve list. This would free up space on the active roster so the coach could add another player while keeping Carl on reserve.

Faking an injury would require Carl to lie to team doctors. Carl thought back to the knee injury he'd suffered at Vanderbilt. That could have been a career ender, but we believed God had enabled him to completely heal from that injury. Each day after Carl joined the NFL, we trusted God for strength and protection from injury. Faking an injury would have gone against everything we had been asking of God.

We sought advice from trusted friends, with mixed results. What was clear to us, though, was that Carl's future with the team hinged on his decision. Even knowing that refusing to fake an injury would likely mean being released and replaced on the roster—and the paychecks ending immediately—we had no doubt it was the right decision to make.

We also knew that doing the right thing would cost us.

Carl told his coach he would not fake an injury and was promptly released. The silver lining in a very dark cloud was that we were able to move back to our hometown of Valdosta, Georgia, with our newborn son, Kyle.

OFF THE ROLLER COASTER

I knew better than to expect that having a baby would automatically make our marriage better. But I didn't anticipate how much more dependent on Carl I would become.

Following Carl's release from the Bengals, I hoped that Carl would give up on football and focus on using his Vanderbilt degree to provide for our family. I would catch myself picturing a life in which Carl held a "normal" job and our income no longer depended on whether a team would pick him up or keep him on its roster.

Carl wasn't envisioning the same future. He couldn't let go of his football dream and bounced around from team to team, trying to catch on with a permanent roster spot, even when I became pregnant with our second child. When Carl's NFL options seemed to have dissipated, he entertained joining the World League of American Football (WLAF).

We had no health insurance, because neither of us had a job. We were living with my parents on the farm where I grew up. Then Carl received a really nice job offer in pharmaceutical sales from a company in Nashville. To me, the decision was clear. Our family needed Carl to take the Nashville job. For Carl, the decision was clear, too—but it wasn't the decision I wanted him to make.

He knew he had an opportunity to play in the World League, but he didn't yet know with which team. It could have been with a team as close as Orlando, Florida, or Birmingham, Alabama. Or it could have been with one of the league's teams in Europe. Carl didn't care where he played as long as he could continue playing.

I arranged for Carl and me to meet with our pastor. I hoped that together, the pastor and I could talk some sense into him. But my hopes that Carl would choose our family over football were dashed early in the meeting.

"This is a great opportunity," Carl told the pastor. "God's giving me a second chance."

Soon after that meeting, Carl learned that opportunity would be with a team in Sacramento, California. The money wouldn't be great, but he was excited to have a team wanting him to play for them.

Standing outside at the farm, I begged Carl to reconsider.

"I'm going," he told me. "Y'all don't have to go with me, but I'm going."

My heart sank. I was too hurt to say even a word in response.

By this time, our second child, Collin, had come along. He was only a few weeks old. Kyle was still in diapers. And now my husband was preparing to leave for California. Carl wanted us to go with him—he made that clear. I thought I knew what would happen if the boys and I didn't move to California, but I never asked.

I wondered what had happened to the life I'd dreamed about when we married: having a husband with a normal job and knowing when he would be coming home to help with the children. That's what I wanted. I felt as if all Carl's focus was devoted to being a successful athlete, and that he was willing to sacrifice whatever it took to meet that desire. I had no doubt that Carl loved me and the boys, and I also understood his connection to football came because the sport had provided his identity for most of his life.

Still, I grew to resent everything about football.

I'd get out of bed in the middle of the night, take my pillow into the bathroom, lock the door, and press the pillow against my face and scream as hard as I could. I'd beg God to change Carl's mind, to help him love me and the boys enough to put aside his dream of continuing to play football.

I saw no signs of my requests being answered.

In the end, I believed the only way to keep our family together was to move to California with Carl. God blessed us even in that move. We made wonderful friends in California and Carl excelled with the Sacramento Surge. His team won a World Bowl—the WLAF's version of the Super Bowl. During his final season in Sacramento, our third son, Kendal, was born.

In 1994, when Kendal was one, Carl decided to walk away from the game he loved. I appreciated how difficult that was for him, and my heart broke seeing his agony over the realization that his playing days were over. In all honesty, though, I was thrilled and relieved about what this meant for our family moving forward.

Carl landed a pharmaceutical sales job in Georgia, and Cara completed our family in 1995. Carl's job eventually moved us to Jacksonville. Our four kids were ages three to nine, and it was a good time for us to settle into one place. We built our first home. Our kids were near both our families. We had begun to heal, and the move to Jacksonville represented a fresh start for us. I could feel a sense of normalcy in our lives.

As much as I had enjoyed the perks of being married to an athlete, I looked forward to us no longer riding the waves of victories and losses. We could count on consistent paychecks. For the first time in our marriage, I felt secure because our livelihood no longer was handcuffed to roster decisions.

Finally, our family could escape the emotional roller coaster of athletics.

CHAPTER 4

SEASON OF CHANGE

If a white picket fence represents the ideal American family life, our family after Carl retired from playing football is best illustrated by a chain-link fence—like the type that surrounds ball fields.

When Kyle had turned five, while Carl was still playing football, we'd signed him up for his first organized sport, baseball. Because Kyle was our oldest, Carl had included him in his professional sports experience. He'd perch Kyle on his broad shoulders after games and carry him to the locker room, and Kyle would remain on his shoulders as his dad conducted postgame interviews with the media.

We bought Kyle his own helmet when he was about three. When we attended Carl's games, Kyle watched intently, running up and down the stadium stands along with the action on the field. When we watched games on TV, Kyle wore a full football uniform and his helmet. Each play, he'd wait for the snap of the ball on the screen and then run around the living room, acting out his own plays.

As soon as Kyle started playing baseball, and then flag football the following year, he showed natural athletic ability and instinct. He stood out among the other kids in his understanding of the game and for the intensity with which he played. Not surprisingly, Collin and Kendal also took to organized sports as soon as they were old enough.

Oh my gosh, I recall thinking. *We're starting all over again.*

Cara was almost six years younger than Kyle and the first girl on my side of the family. My parents had fourteen grandsons when Cara came along. Carl and I hoped having a girl would mean a change from all sports, all the time. Nothing against female sports at all, because we probably just assumed life would be different.

We should have known better.

Carl and I were heartbroken when we enrolled Cara in dance classes at age four and she announced to us, "I'm not that kind of girl. I want to play ball." It wasn't just that our kids played sports, but all four possessed an intense desire to play.

Against my hopes following Carl's retirement, I had to come to grips with the realization that not only were we going to be spending most of our family time at ball fields, but that once again our lives would revolve around the ups and downs of sports.

I assumed that being by my husband's side, encouraging him while he played college and professional ball, had prepared me better than the average mom for the world of youth sports. I had no idea that being the mom of athletes would prove more difficult than being the spouse of one.

Like any parent, I wanted our children to succeed at whatever they decided to pursue. When all four chose athletics, Carl and I became their biggest fans. Just like other parents, we derived much joy from watching our children perform. But when they chose sports, their performances were no longer a private audition for us, their proud parents, in the comfort and solitude of our family room. Instead, they entered a very public arena that exposed them to the acceptance or rejection of a world eager to judge their performances. I knew from

Carl's experience as an athlete what lay ahead, but I had no idea how difficult it would be or how heart-wrenching it would be to see my children experience public failure. Still, there we were, with four kids who wanted nothing more than to be just like their dad—an athlete.

Carl and I ensured that our kids received the best athletic opportunities, and we went overboard. Before buying our home in Jacksonville, Carl surveyed the athletic programs offered by various communities, even researching what types of offense each high school football team ran. Kyle was only nine. He wasn't in junior high yet, and we made a major family decision based partly on varsity offensive schemes.

We spared no expense in securing the best training for our kids' athletic development. We spent our finances, energy, and time at ball fields. We didn't take family vacations, unless you count tournaments as vacations. We just hoped the tournaments would be in nice locations. We missed funerals, weddings, and family reunions because of sports.

Each season seemed more important than the previous one, and thus, more intense. Our kids were standout athletes, and we could already see their potential to play beyond high school. Missing a game, let alone a practice, was not an option. Carl and I disagreed about that. I would express my belief that it was okay to attend church or a family event instead of a game or practice, but Carl would counter that it was crucial for the kids' development to be at *every* game and practice. There's a coach's saying: When an athlete takes a day off, the competition gets better than him. That was the unstated philosophy in our house. I remember once when Kyle was so sick with a fever that he could hardly get out of bed. I gave him medicine and took him to his baseball game, then felt guilty while cheering him on.

I'm not complaining about my husband—I was either for or went along with every decision. Our way of living was not out of line with our circle of friends, either. We hung out with people who also spent much of their time and effort on their kids' sports. We were doing what we thought would provide the best opportunities for our kids.

Still, it became painfully clear in later years that Carl and I were sending the wrong message: that athletic performance was more important than anything or anyone else. And it wasn't as if we didn't know better when we were in the middle of it. We did. We made those decisions anyway. Our kids wanted to play sports with a high level of commitment, and we wanted to give them what they wanted. They were thriving in their sports, and that fed into our mind-set. We allowed our kids to trek down a path from which there was no return.

AT WHAT COST?

Our family reached a crisis point as Kyle neared high school. We had recently built a new home when Carl lost his job as part of a corporate downsizing. For me, the next step was obvious: Carl would get another sales job and we could continue with the status quo. Carl had a different plan. He had devoted countless hours to teaching and training our kids in their respective sports. When he lost his job, he told me he wanted to become a coach at a local high school, where he could coach football and our boys.

A switch from pharmaceutical sales to coaching would mean a significant decrease in pay. I thought Carl was being selfish. His salary reduction would force us to sell the new home that I adored, I would have to find a full-time job to make ends meet, and our lives once again would revolve around wins and losses.

I believed I had made enough sacrifices for Carl's career. I had supported us financially while he played college football. I had supported him during his NFL days when I believed he was more concerned about football than our marriage. I had moved with Kyle and Collin to California when he chose to play in the World League against my pleas to give up football for our family's sake. I anticipated that Carl would make the decision to change careers regardless of how I felt about it.

I unloaded on Carl, threatening through angry tears to leave him.

For weeks after the outburst, I seriously considered divorcing him. I probably would have if not for my experiences around other parents at our kids' ball games. I'd seen several of our kids' teammates whose parents had divorced, and I had sadly noted how negatively divorce affected the children.

I sank into depression. I tried to come up with ways that I could escape the situation. I recognize now how completely false these thoughts were at the time, but I told myself that if I was no longer a part of my family's lives, they would continue on with their lives and be happy. My depression deepened, and I developed suicidal thoughts. I thought Carl and the boys would be fine without me. But I couldn't deny that Cara would not be okay. That's why—thank God—I never acted on those thoughts. I had a good friend whose mother had committed suicide. She often told me stories about her mother and how much she missed and needed her mom in her life. I knew that Cara needed me to be her mom. More than that, she needed me to be a *strong* mom. I'd been a pushover for far too long. I hadn't always given in to Carl, but I had on too many occasions.

That's when I met the strong mentor I desperately needed—Kathy Cope, who not only helped me through that time in my life, but also become a significant part of our effort to put the football field in Barrow. Kathy was a strong woman with a great marriage and great kids. To that point in my life, I'd taken the concept of a submissive wife to a wrong extreme. In Kathy, I found a mentor who demonstrated how a woman could be God-honoring, a good wife and mom, and a strong woman. Those qualities would prove invaluable for what I was called to do with the project.

This also was around the time when I'd made that middle-of-the-night discovery about my personality while studying *40 Days of*

Purpose. I was beginning to understand better how God had wired me. Between that realization and Kathy's help, I began focusing on becoming the strong woman, wife, and mom that I believed God wanted me to be. That I knew Carl and my kids needed me to be.

SHOW OF SUPPORT

With time and through much prayer, I was able to take a step back and clearly evaluate what truly was important about Carl: he loved me and our children. He spent as much time as possible with our kids, helping them grow in their passions—and they appreciated having a dad who could coach them. Carl and I had been together since high school. When he suffered a major injury in college, I was by his side nursing him back to health. In the lowest of his lows in professional football, when he wondered if he'd have to give up the sport because there would be no next team offering the next opportunity, I was there encouraging him.

I had filled the same role for Kyle, Collin, Kendal, and Cara. From their first days in sports, I had encouraged them to persevere and overcome challenges, to not only endure adversity but to grow because of it. I created parenting opportunities out of sports, teaching the kids the importance of every word they spoke. When they struggled on the field, I would teach them that their words were powerful and impacted their performance.

Now I needed to offer the same for my husband. He needed my support.

And what our marriage needed most was for me to work on myself instead of trying to change Carl. He *had* changed. He no longer wanted to move around the country for football. He wanted to settle down together as a family. I considered that perhaps God had placed this change in Carl's heart. True, Carl wouldn't be making the money he had before, but maybe coaching was what God had created Carl to do. All those years of playing football might have been God's way of preparing him to coach.

One day I prayed, *God, I'm going to trust you and let you make my husband into who You want him to be, not who I want him to be.*

When I took that step of beginning to trust God, our marriage began to heal at a rate like never before.

It wasn't long before Carl received an opportunity we could not have anticipated. St. Johns County offered Carl a job as assistant director of Parks & Recreation that would provide schedule flexibility to coach high school football in the afternoons. He was also hired as offensive coordinator for the Bartram Trail High School football team.

Putting the house up for sale pained me. We started looking for a rental home, and I gave Carl one stipulation: I did not want to rent in the same neighborhood as our home, because I didn't want to see anyone else living in the house I had designed for our family. We looked and looked and looked. The only rental we could find was five doors down from our home. I knew this wasn't a coincidence, but a lesson I needed in humility and trusting God.

I also had to step outside of my comfort zone and take a full-time sales job. I would have to grow in that job and in confidence, because Carl's career change propelled our family into a new chapter of our lives—one I never saw coming.

CHAPTER 5

MEN BUILT FOR OTHERS

Darrell Sutherland was a godsend for our family. He started the Bartram Trail High School football program when the school opened in 2000, and he was the one who hired Carl as an assistant coach. I had no idea how much Coach Sutherland would impact not only our sons as their head coach, but also Carl.

And me.

We had heard that Coach Sutherland promoted character development and didn't evaluate his teams based only on victories. Frankly, that is said about many coaches and programs, and it's not always accurate. We all know how that works. Leadership in every program says they are concerned about hiring coaches who develop young people of character, but if those coaches don't produce winning seasons, they don't seem to stay around long. On the flip side, there could be a head coach who everyone knows has bad character and won't produce anything other than winning seasons. For those coaches, the bad things seem to get overlooked because they're winning. We all have seen such extremes.

But after Carl began coaching at Bartram Trail, it didn't take long for us to see that Coach Sutherland's reputation was accurate. If anything, the good reports we'd heard about him might have been understated. He also seemed to have the ability to lead a winning program.

Coach Sutherland taught from a curriculum titled "Men Built for Others," aiming to develop players who would win on and off the football field. He assigned each coach a different attribute to speak on each week. Carl often told me how different Coach Sutherland's program was from anything he had experienced in football. He noted how intentional Coach Sutherland seemed about every detail of the program, including off-season conditioning, precise agendas, and structured practices, with character curriculum written into the training schedule. And that character development was just as important as anything the team did on the field or in the weight room.

As a freshman the previous year, Kyle had started at quarterback for a nearby private school. Then he transferred to Bartram, which had a senior quarterback who had also started the previous season. The coaches wanted to place Kyle at running back. But he loved being a quarterback, and he complained loudly at home about his potential new position.

Kyle and I talked about the situation one morning as I drove him to school.

"Mom, I'm better than the other guy," he said. "I need to be playing ahead of him."

Lord, I prayed silently, *give me the words to say to him.*

"Do you remember the story about Joseph in the Bible?" I asked.

"Yeah, that dude whose brothers threw him into the pit," Kyle said.

"You know, Kyle, wherever Joseph was, even when he was in prison, instead of complaining, he did what he had to do with the best of his ability. And God raised him out of that."

As Kyle and I continued to talk, I couldn't gauge how much of my intended message Kyle comprehended. "If Coach Sutherland puts me at running back today," he said, "I'm quitting. I'm walking off."

When Kyle exited the car, he told me, "I might be seeing you early."

I prayed again: *Lord, please work in my son's heart.*

Kyle wasn't known for his patience. Neither was Carl. These types of situations were battles I typically lost. "You just don't understand," I'd be told. "You are not an athlete."

When I got home from work that evening, Kyle wasn't there. *This is a good sign*, I thought. *He's still at practice.*

Carl arrived home before Kyle.

"What happened?" I asked.

"Boy, you'd be so proud of your son," Carl answered. Eager for details, I asked again what had happened.

"They moved him to running back," Carl said. "He had an amazing practice."

When Kyle walked through the door, it was all I could do to keep from asking for his account. So, I waited—a few seconds.

"Coach Sutherland moved me to running back," Kyle said, "and I told him that I was going to be like Joseph and work to the best of my ability no matter where I was put." I was beginning to see something surprisingly different in my son since coming to Bartram. He was gaining a new perspective on football, and he was learning through a combination of football and life we had never experienced.

Under my breath, I thanked the Lord. That was a huge parenting moment for me, to hear that Kyle wanted to follow Joseph's example. It was one of those memories a momma likes to hold on to for years. For me as a parent, it was important to see God speaking to Kyle through his talent in football. We believed that God had blessed each of our children with athletic ability, and we wanted them to be God-honoring in how they competed on the field. But, we can see now, we had made a god out of sports. Yet God used the very thing we had placed ahead of Him to make His presence known to us.

In that Friday night's game, Kyle accounted for four touchdowns: one rushing, two receiving, and one passing. The senior quarterback starting ahead of him was injured a couple of games later, and Kyle took his place. The time spent at running back benefited Kyle's game when he moved back to quarterback, because it made him more confident running the ball. I believe God was preparing Kyle to become not only a more complete quarterback, but also a more complete person. Sports was Kyle's passion, and God had shown He could touch him through sports.

We were grateful to have a head coach who believed that football and faith could work hand in hand, and who used the sport to teach important life lessons.

When the team huddled around Coach Sutherland after games, he would ask, "What is our job as coaches?" The players would answer, "To love us!" Then he'd ask, "What is your job?" The players would respond, "To love each other!" The first time I heard that, as odd as it sounded for a football huddle, it also made this momma feel good to know that her sons—and her husband—were learning daily from this new style of leadership.

Coach Sutherland also insisted that his football players serve others on campus. He recognized that being on a football team placed players in positions to lead among their peers. Along with that, being a football player carried responsibilities. Almost every evening, Carl would come home and share with me some piece of wisdom that Coach Sutherland had said to the players that day. Or specific tasks he would assign them to learn how to recognize opportunities to serve. Carl had been around coaches with admirable values, but as a part of Coach Sutherland's staff, he made sure to tell me how affirmed he felt about changing professions and to assure me that our boys were benefiting from being a part of the Bartram program.

My original resistance to Carl taking a salary cut to enter coaching transformed into a growing excitement over an environment in which sports was treated with a perspective more in line with what I desired for our family.

COACHING AS MINISTRY

I was softening to the thought that the Bartram program was different. But what would happen if Coach Sutherland faced a choice that would cost him a win or a winning season? I wasn't convinced the program would pass that test.

But I soon found out.

In Carl's first season at Bartram, the Bears won their first district championship in the program's history. They had made the playoffs four times previously, but they had yet to win a postseason game. That year's team had a great chance to end that drought.

Before each season, every player signed a character contract that Coach had put together, with a list of expectations for the players and how they would represent their school and team. Abstaining from alcohol was on the list. That year, the homecoming game was late in the season, and Coach Sutherland had received a report that several football players had been drinking alcohol at the homecoming dance.

At Monday's practice following homecoming, Coach confronted the team and asked that those who had been drinking come forward. None did, and the players continued practice seemingly unaffected. Carl was disappointed in the players, but business carried on as usual.

Tuesday was a different story.

I came home from work to see Carl's and the boys' trucks in the driveway. That never happened during football season. Something was wrong. Bad wrong.

Carl was in the bedroom. The boys followed me down the hallway, stopping outside the door as I entered.

"What's going on?" I asked.

"Close the door," he said, visibly upset.

Carl waited until the door was shut to continue. "Our season is over. When we got to practice today, there was a note in the locker room telling everyone to turn in their equipment because the season was over."

"Did you talk to Coach?" I asked.

"Of course I tried, but he was not going to waver on the issue."

"Do you think it's fair to punish the whole team because of a few knuckleheads?" I asked.

"Even I hate to admit it," Carl said, "but our team is finally buying into working together as a team and not just selfishly trying to be in it for themselves. I sure hope that Coach's decision somehow works. I want to support him in his decision, but this is tough."

What is this? Choosing to do the right thing over winning? Could it be?

The seriousness of the players' actions and the strength of Coach's response placed Carl in a position where he couldn't sit on the fence on the issue. He hadn't faced a decision like this since he'd chosen to do the right thing over the potential cost when a coach wanted him to fake an injury.

On one hand, Carl didn't consider it fair that the entire team should have to suffer because a few had broken team rules. He had two sons on the team that were having the rest of their season wiped out for something they were no part of. But on the other hand, he respected the fact that Coach Sutherland refused to waver from the program's guiding principles in a difficult situation. Carl recognized that if the Bartram football program was going to be what the coaches and players said it would be, then this was an opportunity to take a bold stand for the program's principles.

By Thursday, the players who had been drinking, or at least some of them, had admitted their involvement. The season was back on, but the team didn't practice again before the next game. Instead, coaches and players held a come-to-Jesus meeting that day, with everything placed on the table. Players and coaches alike searched their souls. A few of the coaches opened up to the players about mistakes they had made in their lives. Players realized the lessons they were learning from the episode, and they felt free to openly express themselves. That was a big deal for teenage boys. The frank discussion strengthened the players' bond as teammates, and from that experience, they started referring to themselves as the "Band of Brothers."

That meeting turned out to be a defining moment for that team and the Bartram Trail teams that followed. For a young coach in a young program, a precedent had been set: the rules in place would be followed or there would be serious consequences. No cost—including losing a game or canceling a season—was too great to preserve the standards that every player understands and accepts before a season starts.

Based on what I observed and what Carl and our boys told me, I have no doubt that if those players hadn't confessed to drinking, Coach Sutherland would have forfeited the remaining games. He is a man of principle, and he is strong enough to stick with his convictions.

This team was different from any I'd been around. From that point on, I was all in on my husband's decision to coach at Bartram.

IMPACT AT HOME

Coach Sutherland's teachings began manifesting in the actions of my boys and Carl. Kyle and Collin looked for students sitting alone at lunch so they could sit beside them and befriend them. They and other boys on the team started picking up trash on campus instead of walking past it, taking responsibility for keeping their campus clean instead of viewing it as someone else's job. It was common to observe players walking from the main school building to the field house for practice and picking up trash along the route.

Carl also looked for ways to serve. He invited players to our home to watch game film with him so he could spend more time with them. When he asked if I would mind feeding a group of players dinner once a week, I said I would be glad to do it. I was already cooking for six, so what was another plate or two? That's what led to our Thursday night dinners with up to eighteen players in our home during football season.

It was through those dinners that I witnessed the biggest impact the Bartram program was making on my husband.

Those dinners were more about relationships than about football. All of us would gather in the kitchen, hold hands, and pray for blessings over the food and the lives of the young men. Thursday night became an opportunity for the players to talk about whatever was on their minds. We laughed a lot too. Strong bonds formed between Carl and the boys as he became not only a coach, but a male role model. Some of those players desperately needed that, because they did not have fathers in their homes. Even for those who did have solid dads, the influence Carl and the other coaches carried was huge with the amount of time the players spent with their coaches.

Carl had always invested his time in our kids' athletic endeavors. Now Carl was choosing to do for others' kids what he had been doing for ours. The affirmation came when Carl received a note from a woman thanking Carl for being what she called the only male influence in her grandson's life.

Xavier Brewer was one of my favorite young men we hosted. Xavier was in Kyle's class, and I jokingly referred to him as "the bottomless pit" because he could devour his meal and then clean out any leftovers in the refrigerator. He was the primary reason there was no food left for Cara when she came home. Xavier frequently stayed with his teammates' families, including ours on many occasions. As far as we were concerned, he was one of ours. Our boys picked up Xavier and his younger brother each morning and took them to school. If Kyle went to a football camp, so did Xavier. Once, Carl arranged to take Xavier with Kyle to a summer football camp at Florida State University. When Carl and Kyle went to pick up Xavier, Xavier said he couldn't go because he didn't have the money. Carl was not going to allow Xavier to miss the opportunity to showcase his football skills.

"You've got fifteen minutes to get your stuff together," Carl told him. Xavier did go to the camp with Kyle, and Florida State was the first team to offer Xavier a scholarship.

Xavier needed a strong, caring man like Carl in his life. And Carl needed young men like Xavier to mentor so he could put into practice his emerging view of sports offering a way for him to make a difference in his players' lives.

I was watching another miracle take place. My husband was changing. My kids were changing. *I was changing.* We were impacting others' lives. And to my surprise, God was using a coach and the game of football to bring about the change in all of us.

I could finally start letting go of that resentment toward football I'd held since early in our marriage.

AN APPROACH TO SPORTS WORTH SHARING

Before Carl started coaching at Bartram, we were *that* family when it came to sports. Our reputation was that our kids were very good athletes and they were going to receive opportunities in sports because their dad would make sure they did. Carl wasn't the type of dad content to sit back and watch—he was hands-on in our kids' sports careers. Too hands-on. He thought he was being a good dad by providing what he did not have as a youngster. Carl never knew his biological father. The man who married his mom and adopted Carl was a great dad to Carl. He did everything he could to help Carl in sports, but he hadn't played sports. He was limited. Carl had played football at the highest level. He was able to teach our kids. But his good intentions sometimes got lost in his actions. Carl admits now, and regrets, that he was the dad that coaches hated to have hovering over their kids' teams.

Carl also had been a hothead when it came to watching our kids in sports, and he had been thrown out of so many youth-level games as a coach that it embarrassed me. Almost without fail, when my parents would come to visit and they'd come along to enjoy watching one of their grandkids play a game, Carl would get mad at an umpire and be ejected from the game. I'd get so upset and try to talk to Carl about it at home, but he would argue that it wasn't his fault, that his anger was justified because the umpire had made a bad call.

Even with the changes I could see in Carl after joining the Bartram staff, he still had some work to do on his coaching style. In one game I'll never forget, Kyle threw an interception, and when he returned to the sideline, Carl, as the offensive coordinator, started yelling at him. It was so bad that everyone in the stands got quiet and listened. Carl's every word could be heard, and he wasn't saying, "That's okay, buddy; you'll get 'em next time." Other parents looked over to me in the stands and shook their heads. I was equally livid and embarrassed and told Carl at home, "Don't you ever talk to my son like that again. You have embarrassed me. I can't believe he doesn't hate you."

It was horrible, and I called Coach Sutherland to see if I could solicit his support on the incident. Coach diplomatically told me it was difficult to coach a son, especially when the son plays such a crucial position as Kyle did. I was upset that Coach didn't get mad at Carl—at least that I could hear. But even that was a learning moment for Carl, because Coach could have taken the easy way out by appeasing me and saying he'd talk to Carl. Instead, he struck the delicate balance between not excusing Carl's behavior and demonstrating to Carl that, as his boss, he had Carl's back.

Thankfully, things have changed over the years. Now, when Carl is on the sideline, he calms other people down and reminds the players to stay focused regardless of what is going on around them. Under Coach Sutherland, Carl discovered that he had a purpose in coaching. At Bartram, football stopped being all about winning for Carl.

It became his ministry, an opportunity to use his talents to impact young men.

The Bartram Trail football program changed our family, because it taught us how to put sports in the proper perspective and then provided us with avenues to use our talents to serve others. I had seen the very worst effects that sports could have on people, and I had experienced them to the point that I was ready to end my marriage. Then, Coach Sutherland's leadership demonstrated the good that can come when sports are kept in their proper position.

Now, as I considered next steps in the Barrow project, I realized that we had something worth sharing. We could change lives in Barrow if we could give them a program like ours.

CHAPTER 6

INTRODUCTION TO BARROW

I walked across the room toward Coach Sutherland, chuckling as I watched him busily help his wife, Mary, get their three young children seated before the start of our football team's end-of-season banquet. The scene was typical of Coach: always involved with his family, even when fully engaged in his role as Coach Sutherland.

I wanted to be respectful of his family time as I reached out to hand him a binder I had spent hours preparing for him. Coach led his program in an intentional, meticulous manner, and I'd anticipated having to sell my field idea to him. The marketing packet I'd made for him included details about Barrow, photos of the Whalers' field, a map, articles about the town's social struggles, and a transcript of the ESPN story we had watched. His support was too important to not put in that level of effort. I knew that Carl had told Coach about what we had watched on ESPN and that I wanted to talk to him about getting our school involved to help. The banquet would not be the time and place to discuss the school's potential involvement, so the packet would need to make a good first impression so he would read through it later.

"Coach, I'd like you to take this home and look over it," I told him. I didn't get to start my second sentence.

Without even opening the binder, Coach said, "Cathy, we've been telling our players over and over again that their ability to play football is a gift and should be used to serve others. Now you are presenting us with an opportunity to do what we have been teaching."

Then he *really* shocked me.

"Raising money to give them a football field is not enough. We need to bring them to Jacksonville."

"Yes!" I said. "I was thinking that we could help train their coaches."

"I am talking about training their whole team—players and coaches," Coach Sutherland said. "We need to have them come to Jacksonville and stay in the homes of our players to see what it is like to be a student athlete. They need to be a part of our team's families, eat and study together, and then we can practice football together."

My mental calculator worked overtime as he talked. We already needed to raise an estimated $500,000 to put a field in Barrow. I constantly battled concerns over whether we could raise that large of an amount. Bringing the team to Florida would represent a whole new ball game. A greater expense would require more buy-in from the community than I had planned. I'd no longer be asking people to just donate money, but also to invest their time in the Barrow team.

I asked Coach, "Do we need to add the cost of bringing them to Florida to the expense of what is needed for the field?"

"No," he answered. "Let them purchase their airline tickets to get down here, and then we can handle all the rest."

I could handle "all the rest." *This will be easy*, I thought.

After the banquet, I excitedly shared my conversation with my family. I knew Coach was a must for rallying community support, but

I hadn't anticipated how much influence his support would carry at home. My family—especially Carl—had been lukewarm to my crazy idea, but now they were beginning to at least consider it as probable. I was glad, because our family would need to be heavily involved in a trip to Jacksonville for the Barrow coaches and players.

On top of paying for a field north of the Arctic Circle, I now had taken on bringing a high school team from the tip-top of Alaska all the way to Florida—from one corner of the country to the opposite corner. The idea was growing. The financial need and resources were increasing. So were my responsibilities.

Yet I still had not talked to anyone from Barrow.

I knew from the ESPN story that Trent Blankenship was superintendent of the North Slope Borough School District, and that it had been his decision to start the Barrow football program following the students' survey. I had been unsuccessful in locating a phone number for the school district, so one day, as I was updating Carl's mother on the phone, I asked if she could help me find a number. She called back with a phone number in the 907 area code. I laughed because it was close to our own area code, 904, in Jacksonville.

I called the number and reached a utility company in Barrow. I told the person who answered that I was trying to contact the school superintendent and asked for help finding his number. She gave me another number, and when I called it, I got Trent's voice mail. I left a message and did not hear back. That was in November.

I called probably a dozen times over the next several weeks, each time leaving a message. On a few of the calls, I said that I was trying to reach him because I wanted to help the football program. None of my calls were returned. After one such fruitless phone call to Barrow, I thought, *Okay. This is going to be more difficult than I thought.*

My excitement at the thought of the Barrow players having a new, green field to play on never waned. But the enormity of the task sank in more and more as I continued to fail to connect with the superintendent. After working part-time before Carl's job change and pay decrease, I now was working full-time selling postage equipment for a paper handling equipment company. Carl was working two jobs, with the Parks & Rec and with the school. We had four teenagers, all neck-deep in sports. We were living almost paycheck to paycheck.

I began to doubt myself. Had I taken on a task that was more than I could handle?

ONE LAST ATTEMPT

The longer I went without talking to the superintendent in Barrow, the more defeated I felt. While driving to a sales call one day in early January, it hit me that if I couldn't get the receiving end of what we were working on to get on board with the idea, then I was wasting my time and effort. I saw the need for a field in Barrow. But without having talked to anyone there, I couldn't know for sure Barrow wanted a new field. Or perhaps, I thought (and hoped), someone else was ahead of me with the idea. It had been three months since the ESPN story aired. That was more than enough time for another group of people to start working on putting a field in Barrow. Wouldn't that explain why I hadn't received a phone call back?

I desperately needed to connect with the superintendent and confirm the need I assumed Barrow had—but I couldn't figure out how. The time had come to either know that Barrow was on board or pull the plug on the idea once and for all.

I pulled into a McDonald's parking lot and parked under a shade tree. It was late afternoon in Jacksonville, so late morning in Barrow. I'd be busy making dinner and talking with my family that evening. I only had a work number for the superintendent, so I'd have to call during his work hours rather than at night.

This was the best time to call.

I closed my eyes and prayed, *Okay, Lord. I'm going to give this one more shot. If they don't answer this time, then this was not You. If this is You, Lord, they have to answer this time when I call.*

I called up the superintendent's number one last time, clearing my throat as I dialed. Trent quickly answered. I was shocked!

"Hey, there. My name is Cathy Parker," I excitedly said, "and I'm a coach's wife and football mom from Jacksonville, Florida."

Trent chuckled. "Well, hello," he said. "I can certainly tell that you are from the South, with that Southern accent."

I laughed. "I know. I can't deny it."

I told Trent that I was calling because of the ESPN story about the football program. "It's awesome what you are doing," I said. "Have you gotten a lot of response from people who saw the show?"

"Yes, we have!" he replied.

I commended the school for what the football program was accomplishing. Trent was kind in his comments and didn't seem rushed to end the call and move on to his next order of business. I actually sensed a little excitement in his voice at receiving my call.

Learning that others had also been moved to action encouraged me, yet I also waited—and wished—for Trent to tell me that someone more qualified than me had stepped up to bring a new field to the program. This would not only validate my idea; it would also remove the pressure from me to make it happen.

"Have people been offering to help y'all?" I asked.

The phone connection had been lagging. I was wondering if Trent was still on the call when he answered the question.

"Oh, yes," he said. "We have been amazed at the response and calls."

"How have people offered to help?"

"Well, they have called and encouraged us."

"Has anyone offered to give y'all an artificial turf field to play on?"

I heard nothing for several seconds. Had I lost the connection? "Well, no," Trent finally replied, dragging out his response.

When I heard that response, I dove right into the deep end of the pool. "That is what I am calling to tell you," I informed him. "We are currently putting an artificial turf field in our community in Florida, and God has put it on my heart to give one to your community as well."

"You're an angel!" Trent immediately responded. "I have been thinking we needed to take our team to the Lower 48 to learn more about playing football."

My smile grew wider at hearing another person independently suggest the idea.

"We are the lowest state of the 48, and we know football!" I joked/boasted. "And that was the next thing I wanted to tell you: our football team wants to have your team come to Florida, stay in our homes, and learn football."

"You've got to be kidding," he said.

After I assured him I was serious, we chatted for a few more minutes. Then I asked why he hadn't returned my phone calls.

"I didn't know you called," he said.

"I've been leaving messages."

"Oh, I never check my messages."

I rolled my eyes. The frustration over not connecting with Barrow had caused me to doubt whether the idea was something I was supposed to act on. I was within one unanswered call of completely abandoning the mission—all because my voice mails went unchecked.

INTO THE CONTROVERSY

Unbeknownst to me, Trent informed an assistant football coach, Brian Houston, of our conversation. Both agreed not to tell anyone, because even as far-fetched as the field idea seemed, once anyone else found out about the possibility, hopes would raise sky-high. If the field didn't come through—and at that early stage, that seemed the most likely outcome—the program would suffer from the disappointment.

Still, somebody told someone, because as I learned later, the whole town knew by the next day. That included the only radio station in Barrow, which called me to request a phone interview.

Other than Trent, the only other person in Barrow I'd spoken with was the person at the utility company who answered when I called the wrong number. That was it. I didn't know—I *couldn't* know—that I and the field idea were already being met with skepticism by the residents of Barrow. Accepting the interview request brought my first taste of the controversy surrounding the football program.

The show's host followed what I considered a negative line of questioning during the interview because I wasn't from Barrow and had never even been to Alaska.

"You have nothing in common with us," she told me.

"You're wrong," I answered. "I do. And it's our greatest resource: our young men. We're trying to build great young men here, and you're trying to build great young men there."

I could hear through the phone the host's tone toward me begin to mellow. But I had no way of knowing just how much that answer had changed opinions toward me among her audience.

CHAPTER 7

OBEDIENCE PLUS INSPIRATION

Susan Hope and I connected from our first conversation. Susan was Trent's secretary, and after a few phone calls with Trent in which we discussed the possibility of the Barrow team coming to Jacksonville, he introduced me to Susan.

Obedience had driven me in the first three months. As my relationship with Susan quickly developed and she provided me a native's insight into Barrow's culture and heritage, inspiration became an equal motivator.

In our first conversation, Susan and I discovered we both were in our early forties and we were mothers of high school athletes. She loved to talk as much as I did. Susan told me that, like Trent, she had a son, Jarid, on the football team.

"What position does he play?" I asked.

"He's a point guard," she answered.

I laughed and thought her son must also play basketball. I asked

Susan a few more questions and discerned that he probably was a lineman.

Susan described the opportunities football had created for native boys. Barrow offered high-paying jobs to attract workers from outside of the area. In high-demand fields such as medicine and education, housing was used to entice people to move to Barrow and work. Move-ins from the Lower 48 typically were more experienced than natives in basketball, giving them an advantage in the competition for starting positions. You weren't going to find Barrow boys honing their skills outside year-round on a driveway basketball goal. But by comparison, the football team, because of its sheer numbers, had more positions to fill, and natives filled many of those spots.

Then Susan told me about how adding the football program had benefited Jarid, specifically. She and her husband had divorced, and Jarid did not have his father around. Susan relished the time that Jarid was around the football coaches, both in season and for off-season workouts. In the absence of Jarid's father, the coaches had served as the father figures Susan believed he needed.

I tried to imagine what it would be like to be in Susan's position—how I would feel if *my* sons were the ones looking for positive male influence from their coaches, much like I witnessed on Thursday nights in our home.

I wouldn't have to convince Susan of how football could change young men's lives.

INTRODUCTION TO THE IÑUPIAT

Before that initial conversation with Susan, the extent of my knowl-edge of Barrow had come from the ESPN story, a few short phone calls with Trent, and my internet research. I knew Susan would be a key contact for me in Barrow. For one, she checked her voice messages! If

I needed to reach Trent, my best shot would be through Susan. With Trent's interest in a trip to Jacksonville for the Barrow team, Susan's role as his secretary placed her in the middle of all I would need to know from the team's end. In addition, Susan was the person who could teach me about the way of life in the North Slope. Unlike Trent, she had been born in Barrow. She hadn't only learned the traditions and customs of the town; she had lived them.

It was through regular talks with Susan that I became fully fascinated with Barrow. Her sweet personality shined through her voice, and it was easy to feel her love for her community and heritage. Her experiences made me realize how much I took for granted as the mother of athletes.

In one conversation, Susan was elated that Jarid came home from football practices so tired that he would eat dinner and go to bed instead of staying up all night playing video games. Getting kids to sleep at night and then be active during the day could be a challenge in Barrow, she told me, because they had months with no sunlight and months with continuous sunlight. Football practices and conditioning transformed the youth's physical activity levels. Our kids had grown up in sports, and I had given little thought to the conditioning associated with sports that was new to many families in Barrow.

Each phone call, Susan told me more about Barrow's culture, and I grew more in awe of the people there. I had always heard the native people of Alaska referred to as "Eskimo." Susan told me that in northern Alaska, the natives were called Iñupiat, and that many in Barrow still spoke the Inupiaq language. In the South, where I was raised, we believed we treated our elders with respect because we said "Yes sir" and "No sir," and called them "Mr." and "Mrs." unless they told us to call them by their first names. I could tell from Susan's stories about her community that respect for elders worked at a higher level among the Iñupiat.

Susan also talked a great deal about her neighbors, because their culture emphasized helping others in need. I guiltily surveyed a mental map of our neighborhood and pictured the houses whose owners we did not know. The way Susan talked, everyone in Barrow knew one another and knew they had to help each other because of the harsh climate and conditions.

Once, I mentioned the negative comments about the football program I had heard in the ESPN story. From growing up in the South, I knew the effects of racism and prejudices. But because everything I was learning about Barrow was so fascinating, I had a difficult time understanding the cultural divides of the people there.

"Do you have these problems with racism and prejudice?" I asked. "Is that why I'm hearing those things? Is it prejudice toward the native people? Because I know what that looks like, and I know how to navigate that."

"You and I are the same age," she said. "But in my lifetime, things have changed more drastically than in yours. When I was a young girl, my job was to take my sled out and bring in a large block of ice for my family as our water for the day. In a thirty-year span, we went from having no indoor plumbing to having satellite systems that track the movement of the whales. Not only has technology changed for us in such a short period of time, but we have so many people move here from all over the world to obtain the high-paying jobs offered in education and health care. These newcomers don't understand the value of living off the land, sea, and air, like the Iñupiat people. We've had an influx of people into our community that has no roads going out of it, and we are all expected to get along. We have to learn to get along. The social problems and the prejudice that you've seen, you've had generations to experience. We've had to experience that in a thirty-year span."

Susan told me the divide developed because people coming in from other cultures didn't understand the Iñupiats' subsistence society and thus didn't honor the Iñupiats' tradition of living off the land, air, and sea. Money had attracted many of the newcomers to northern Alaska, and they preferred to purchase what they needed to live there instead of learning the skills that have upheld the Iñupiat for generations.

The unseen price tag was the Iñupiats' heritage.

APPRECIATING THE HERITAGE

From the start, I had focused on my belief that the Barrow team coming to Jacksonville would serve as a great opportunity for the players at our high school to help the Barrow players, and that our kids would be able to teach them. My conversations with Susan corrected my thinking; it was clear that we—both the players and the parents of Bartram—could also learn from our Alaskan visitors. I had focused on the material things our kids had that the Barrow kids didn't. Instead, I learned through Susan's descriptions of Iñupiat culture that what we considered important in Jacksonville was not necessarily important in Barrow.

With a trip to Jacksonville progressively looking more likely, I called Susan from my office one day to ask pressing questions so I could check boxes on my to-do list. I walked out of my office and into the parking lot, pen and paper in hand for taking notes, so I could get the information I needed, uninterrupted. Susan wanted nothing to do with talk of a potential trip.

"Oh, Cathy, today's the most wonderful day!" she started. "We harvested our first whale of the season. It is so wonderful to see the whole community come together to help pull the whale onto the ice. With the first harvested whale of the season, the captain spearheads a wonderful celebration for the community."

"What kind of celebration?" I asked.

"Well, with the first whale of the season, the captain and his crew cut up the whale," Susan explained. "They give the meat to those who are the neediest—the widows and orphans—first. Then the captain distributes the meat to everyone in the community. We have a great celebration and meal that evening for the whole community."

"That sounds really awesome. Does the captain keep any of the whale meat?"

"No, the first whale of the season is to be shared with the community. What is left over goes to his whaling crew."

I was amazed that the captain would be so generous after all the hard work of capturing a whale.

"We have gotten away from some of our earlier traditions," Susan said. "Years ago, after the big celebration and feast of the first harvest, the captain would open his home to the community to take anything they wanted. The only things the people were not allowed to take were the captain's whaling equipment."

"What do you mean? What types of things were people allowed to take from the captain's home?"

"Everything—except his whaling equipment," she said. "People could take his TV or his clothes. His vehicle."

"But, Susan, people didn't actually take his stuff, did they?"

"Why, yes, Cathy," she responded, apparently surprised I did not understand the tradition. "Because if you are going to hold the honor of being captain of the whaling team—who is the most esteemed person in the community—you have to show that you are willing to give up everything, even your life, for your neighbor."

I could barely speak as I ended the conversation. I went back into my office, weeping. I repeated for a coworker what Susan had told me. The story stunned him. I sat alone in my office, processing what Susan had shared. I thought we in Jacksonville had what the people of Barrow needed, and that we would be giving to them. Yet, we had much to learn from the people of Barrow about the spirit of giving.

Susan had previously told me of the whale's significance in Iñupiat culture, because the whale had sustained them for generations. Whales ate plant-eating fish, so whale meat provided nutrients the Iñupiat could not get on their own because of their inability to grow fruit and vegetables in the frozen tundra. The Iñupiat had previously used oil from whales for heating. They fermented portions of a whale for use as a medicine, called *mikiqiaq*, because the whale had great healing power for natives. She fascinated me with stories of people who were almost on their deathbeds and then were healed when given mikiqiaq because something in the natives' bodies responded to it. "But if *you* ate it," Susan told me, "it would probably kill you."

A nephew of Susan's had not wanted to cut whale meat because the non-native kids at school would make fun of him for smelling like whale. She made clear that no product on the market could remove whale oil smell from clothing. It pained Susan and other natives to see their children disassociate with their heritage, their culture, and their livelihood.

From what I gathered from Susan, starting the football program stirred up differences within the community, which already was dealing with issues caused by its diversity. Much of the debate over football centered on finances. The start of the program was funded through a one-time initiative by the state legislature to keep the youth in school. Because there were no roads out of Barrow, the football team had to fly to its away games. The school also was responsible during its first season for paying for opponents' flights into Barrow—a cost of about $20,000 per home game. Although teachers were paid well in Barrow, before this initiative the school district had turned down an expected increase in teachers' salaries. That added to the controversy. The need to better educate the children of Barrow was not in dispute; the best way to do so was.

Natives were hurt by the opposition to what they viewed as a solution to saving their youth and what remained of their culture.

I believed football could become a unifying factor in Barrow.

I often told Susan of the character curriculum Coach Sutherland employed in our sons' program, saving up stories of small victories involving my sons and from the Thursday night dinners to use to encourage Susan.

The more I told Susan our success stories, and how I had seen my husband mentor young men through football, the more she wanted the same success stories for her son and their community. And the more I wanted to help make them a reality for the people of Barrow. We shared the hope that football would be the tool that would help shape her son and the other young men of Barrow. We knew that the field wasn't the only goal here. It was also imperative that the Barrow team come to Jacksonville so that Coach Sutherland and his staff could mentor their coaches, and their players could learn how Bartram's players handled being students and athletes.

During the life of the project, whenever I came across obstacles and felt discouraged, doubting whether I could handle the task, I'd recall one sentence I'd heard Susan say that kept me motivated:

"We need this program, and we need that field."

CHAPTER 8

IT'S OFFICIAL: PROJECT ALASKA

From Barrow, Trent and Susan talked more optimistically about the football team coming to Jacksonville. At home, momentum for the field idea was gaining strength, with an increasing number of people asking me questions about my idea. I felt a new level of seriousness concerning the field.

The school break for Christmas and New Year's was pretty much the only time of year our family wasn't at a ball field. It was the perfect time for me to work on this project. I had used that time to pick the brains of people I knew had participated in a variety of campaigns, including fund-raising and political campaigns. All were enthusiastic about my idea and encouraged me to move forward.

THE FIRST DONATION

One contact put me in touch with a start-up Rotary Club in our area, St. Johns, and I was invited to visit in January as the club's first guest speaker. "You can't ask for money," I was told. I assured them I would only talk about our plans to place a field in Barrow.

I was forty-one and older than almost every one of the thirty men at that meeting. Armed with stories from Susan, I told them everything I could about Barrow and the field without mentioning I needed their money. As I spoke, the young, successful professionals' eyes were locked on me, their heads nodding. They were clearly moved by the story and our goal of building a field in Barrow.

Afterward, a man named Brad Hill introduced himself as working for SchenkelShultz Architecture. I'd heard of his company but didn't know it was the largest architectural firm for schools in Florida. His company designed schools, ball fields, and practically anything else associated with schools.

"I've had arctic architectural training," Brad said. "Can I help you?"

What are the chances of meeting someone in Florida with arctic architectural training? I wondered.

"Yes, absolutely," I told him.

I had no idea how significant Brad's offer would become.

Another man handed me a check. "This isn't from Rotary. This is from me," he told me. "I want to personally support this."

The check was for $500—our first donation.

We're getting serious now, I realized. And then it dawned on me how far behind I was on the basics I needed for running this project. I didn't even have a nonprofit established for someone to make out a check to. I needed help to successfully run this.

I called upon my mentor, Kathy Cope. Kathy was an amazing businesswoman who had served in the military and could be appropriately direct. Kathy was driven and business-minded, skilled at organization and administration while also conducting her business in an honorable manner. She expertly ran a nonprofit with a mission similar to what we wanted to do in Barrow, and I knew she could help me with the loose ends I hadn't anticipated.

Although Kathy was a close friend—perhaps *because* she was a close friend—I found it difficult to ask her for what I needed: a non-profit organization to accept donations for the Barrow project.

If only she'd offer to help, I thought. I was concerned about putting her on the spot, although I was sure she would have no problem asking me for help if we switched places. But I also didn't know how I could continue without her help. It would be much easier if she would just volunteer, because then it would be her idea, not mine.

Eventually, I developed a plan.

With my sales calls for the day complete, I called Kathy and asked if I could talk with her as soon as she had time. She asked me to meet her at the nail salon where she was getting a manicure. My stomach was in knots as I pulled up a chair next to her. While she had her nails done, I explained how the man at the Rotary had given me money and that I anticipated more people would soon want to contribute.

"I need a nonprofit that could accept donations," I added.

I never came out and asked Kathy for exactly what I needed, yet several times I said something along the lines of, "I don't know how I will do this without help from someone who already has a nonprofit I can partner with."

I hoped Kathy would take the bait.

"Oh, honey," she'd say. "You'll be okay. The Lord will help you."

I thanked her for her encouragement, but walked out of the salon disappointed. *What could my next step possibly be?* I wondered.

A few minutes later, as I was driving home, my phone rang.

"I was thinking about our conversation," Kathy started. "Would you like to use my nonprofit? Would that be a help to you, if I help you with all the admin stuff and we could do a business-as name and set up a bank account?"

I quickly accepted Kathy's offer, with a sigh of relief.

"I didn't know that you needed me," she said.

"Yes, I need you!" I exclaimed.

She laughed and said, "Okay. I can help you with that. All you had to do was ask."

From that point on, Kathy selflessly served as my assistant on the project.

Kathy's willingness to help following my hesitation to ask helped me realize that if I was going to take on a project this big, I had to stop worrying that I might offend someone. Even if it made me uncomfortable, I had to open my mouth and ask for help. I couldn't assume that if people heard me talk about what Barrow needed, they would jump on board. They needed to be asked to help.

We decided on Project Alaska for the nonprofit's name. Trevor Abs, a Bartram assistant coach, set up a website that gave us the capability to solicit and receive donations. The domain for our name was already claimed. We added the word *Turf* for the website and purchased the domain, projectalaskaturf.com.

At that point, I had Coach Sutherland on board for the local support, I had confirmed Barrow's interest through Trent Blankenship, and Brad Hill had offered to help with architectural needs. The roster of people who would become key players in the project continued to systematically appear, as though their arrivals were being orchestrated.

I have the tendency to start moving and then become oblivious to the steps I'm taking. But God was about to slow me down so I would notice the importance of what I was doing.

I told Kathy that on my lunch break, "I'll just stop by the bank and open the account."

At the bank, I handed the executive our paperwork and explained the purpose of the account. The banker told me a story that redirected my day. Her son had dealt with depression and had taken his own life. She told me that the only time she remembered him being happy was when he was part of a team playing ball.

It struck me that with each person who came on board, there would be a story. There'd be a reason he or she was called to action—a reason compelling enough to share that person's time, resources, and talents.

As those stories accumulated, they inspired me. They also solidified the miraculous nature of what we were involved in.

WHAT IS PLAN B?

We still needed an in for transportation, and one finally came through Rotarian Phil Voss, who sent an email about our turf project to fellow Rotarian Tommy Grimes, the founder of a large logistics company called the Grimes Companies. Tommy replied to the email with, "I knew there would be a day that you would be asking me to transport grass." I laughed at their transportation humor and immediately looked forward to working with Tommy.

When we spoke for the first time, Tommy agreed to lend his company's expertise—largely in the capable person of Ike Sherlock, the director of operations—to research options for transporting a field to Barrow. He would then provide me the numbers of people with whom I'd need to speak.

Soon after I connected with Ike, Kyle came home with a business card for Tom Gloe, a division manager with UPS. He had two daughters at Bartram, and one was a classmate of Kyle's. She gave Kyle her dad's business card and said I should call him because he wanted to help. Tom offered UPS's assistance, and I put him in touch with Ike. The project was starting to gain traction publicly, and having the Grimes Companies and UPS involved on the transportation side brought more legitimacy to our project as we continued to raise funds.

The $500,000 figure that Carl, Steve Coleman, and I had come up with during our first meeting had been merely for the turf itself—it had not included the extreme transportation costs. Now we were in January, still with no sense of how much money we would ultimately need to raise. From the outset, my goal had been to have a field in Barrow, ready for play by the start of the Whalers' next season—in August.

My original plan banked on well-known sports companies writing large checks. Through a friend of a friend, I presented a packet to Under Armour. Their response was, "Great idea. Let us know when you're further along. Maybe we can provide some product." I began to question whether we would raise the money the way I had hoped.

A few weeks earlier, Carl and I had attended a Christmas party. Some of our friends from our kids' sports teams were at the party and were talking about opening a bank. Because of my sales background, they wanted me to join them and help bring in capital. I indicated a potential interest in taking on that challenge, so they started recruiting me. In a follow-up conversation with one of the friends, Bert Watson, I mentioned the field project.

"I just really feel like this is the Lord, and this is something that I'm called to do," I said.

Bert was a big thinker. "Cathy, a couple of things," he said. "You need to meet with our PR firm that helps the bank. It's Paul McCormick. Paul can help tell you what to do."

I knew the name, because the McCormick Agency had helped prominent political figures run for office.

"Have you ever talked to Wayne Weaver?" Bert continued.

I laughed. "No, I don't run in those circles."

Wayne Weaver owned the NFL team the Jacksonville Jaguars. Everyone in our area knew Mr. Weaver, as he was called, because of his reputation for being a kind, generous man. Bert told me to write down a phone number.

"He is a great guy," Bert said. "This is his number. Reach out to him."

I called Paul McCormick first, told him that Bert had recommended I talk to him, and asked if we could meet. (Remember: I had learned to ask for help!) Paul said he was very busy but could give me twenty minutes. As I took a seat in his office, I knew time was short, so I sped through the story and all the work I had done and the people and companies who had aligned with us. Paul listened without interrupting.

When I concluded my pitch, I asked, "What do you think?"

"Well, it's either one of two things," he replied. "Either this is the best story that's come across my desk in a very long time, or you're one crazy woman." (Now Paul jokes that it turned out to be both.)

I asked Paul what I needed to do.

"First of all," he said, "you've done a good little grassroots kind of thing, talking to people. But we've got to have a press conference. I'm talking about a big press conference, with a stage, press packets, and the works."

When I heard "press conference," my stomach turned over. I was fine with talking to groups of people who had invited me to speak, but I knew nothing about dealing with media. Once again, the feeling that I was in over my head began to creep back.

I reluctantly agreed with Paul, who said he would handle inviting all the media. My job was to work on who I would have onstage with me, like the architectural firm and the transportation companies involved.

"You need to have all these people giving you credibility onstage," he said.

Then he asked, "What about the Jaguars? Have you reached out to them?"

I had tried to reach their community relations office, but hadn't talked with anyone yet. I said that Bert had given me a number to call Wayne Weaver.

"We need buy-in from the Jaguars," Paul said. "Pick a date for the press conference. And it needs to be on your school's football field."

Press conference? Oh, my! I had never been a part of anything like a big press conference. And at my kids' school? On their football field? Ugh.

I left Paul's office feeling sick to my stomach. I knew that once we held a press conference, there would be no turning back. That once I stepped out publicly on that grand of a scale, I would have to see the project through to completion.

In my car, I dialed the phone number for Mr. Weaver, expecting to leave a message with his office.

"Hello."

I immediately recognized the voice as Mr. Weaver's! I didn't think that Bert would give me Mr. Weaver's *cell* number. I hastily looked for the nearest parking lot to pull into as I thought, *This is my one shot here.*

"Mr. Weaver, I'm so sorry," I began. "I thought I was calling your secretary. I didn't know I was going to get you."

"What do you want?" he asked in a tone suggesting he was trying to figure out exactly who had his cell number.

I introduced myself and told him that I had been trying to reach his community relations office. I told him briefly about Project Alaska and that my research had informed me that the NFL issued grants for similar community-need projects.

"What kind of time frame are we talking about?" he asked.

"We're talking about raising the money this year before the football season starts."

"Well, we don't have time for anything like that," he said. "Getting a community grant would take a lot longer than we have time for."

Mr. Weaver told me that Dan Edwards was the team's senior vice president of communications. "I'll tell Dan that I spoke to you and that the Jaguars will be involved. I'm not going to make any promises right now on what type of involvement, but Dan will work with you."

I mentioned the press conference I would be scheduling, and he said that Dan would attend to represent the Jaguars.

Before our call ended, Mr. Weaver told me, "I think this is great what you're doing. And you can count on the Jaguars to be involved."

Perhaps the most influential man in Jacksonville sports had just joined our team. I lowered my forehead to the steering wheel and prayed, *Thank You, God, for giving me favor with this man.*

CHAPTER 9

"HE'LL PREPARE THEIR HEARTS"

After I started working full-time at my sales job when Carl switched careers, he offered to make breakfast for the family each morning. He might have thought it would be better for the kids if he did. My breakfast goal was to feed the kids enough to sustain them until lunch. Carl wanted to go all out for the kids' breakfasts because he wanted the boys to put on weight for the next football season.

Each morning while Carl prepared breakfast, I did a devotional with the kids. One morning as the date of the press conference neared, before I started the devotion, Kyle said something in front of the family that snatched all our attention.

"What you're trying to do in Alaska is a real good thing," he said. "But Mom, if it doesn't work out, it's going to be so embarrassing."

All I could say in response was, "I know."

That statement crushed me. Kyle was working hard for an opportunity to play in college. His name appeared frequently in the newspapers for his football and baseball accomplishments and the recruiting attention he attracted. And it hit me that his own mother could be on the verge of embarrassing him at a point in his life when the last thing a well-publicized, teenage boy needs his mother to do is screw something up publicly.

Lord, I prayed, *I need You to give me something to tell him. What do I tell him?*

Carl and I have experienced numerous times when we've prayed for a word from the Lord and the Holy Spirit would bring to mind a verse or passage that we've read. I opened my Bible to no place in particular. I looked down to see Acts 10 on the page and began reading aloud the story of Peter and Cornelius.

Cornelius was a God-fearing officer in the Roman army. Cornelius had a vision of an angel telling him to send men to ask Peter to come visit him. The next day, Peter had a vision in which he was told three times to eat the meat of animals considered unclean by Jewish law. Peter was trying to determine what the vision meant when Cornelius's men arrived. The Holy Spirit told Peter that he had sent the men, so Peter invited them inside and to stay with him. Except, Peter didn't know the men were Gentiles, and a Jew entertaining Gentiles in such a manner contradicted Jewish customs. The next day, Peter left with the men to visit Cornelius—another violation of Jewish traditions. Cornelius gathered an audience and asked Peter to preach. During Peter's sermon, the Holy Spirit moved upon all those gathered and all received salvation. Because both men were obedient to their respective visions, that became an important moment in the spread of the gospel in the newly established church. It opened the eyes of believers to God's desire that *all* people hear the gospel message, not only Jews.

As I read that story to the kids, the part of the story that most struck me came in verses 19–20. The Holy Spirit told Peter, "three men are looking for you. So get up and go downstairs. Do not hesitate to go with them, for I have sent them."

I closed my Bible and told Kyle, "This is what the Lord will do for us. If this is God, He'll go before us, and He'll tell people to help us. He'll prepare their hearts. And they'll come on board, and they'll be riding along with us—if this is the Lord."

That statement seemed to help Kyle, I think partly because that wasn't a moment when we said, "This is definitely from God, so we all need to fall in line and follow." Peter trusted the Holy Spirit, and I did too. I had my own occasional doubts about whether what I felt I should do was truly God wanting me to lead this project or just something I wanted. But I did know that *if* this project was God's doing, He would make everything happen. If not, then it would fail, and I would bring embarrassment on the family.

My ultimate focus with the project was on the teens in Barrow. But as that morning's devotion time bluntly reminded me, there was much at stake for my family too. There was too much on the line in Barrow *and* at home for the project to fail.

I would have been foolish to attempt this project in my own strength. God had placed the field on my heart, and I needed to keep obeying the Holy Spirit's direction.

And trust Him to prepare people's hearts ahead of me.

COURAGE TO ASK

I try to be a warm, friendly person. I like people, and I enjoy talking with people. That trait actually caused issues for me in my job selling postage equipment.

I'd come back to my office from an appointment and my boss would ask how the call went.

"Great!" I'd say. "It's a done deal. We should go ahead and order the equipment."

My boss would suggest I wait until I had the signed paperwork in hand. A few times, the sale fell through.

After one such occasion, my boss asked if he could accompany me on an appointment. When we got into the car after the meeting, he asked, "So, what do you think your chances are of getting that sale?"

"I think I've got it!" I confidently answered.

My boss looked me in the eyes and said, "Cathy, you can't believe everything people say. The only reason that person did not come straight out and tell you no is because people don't have the heart to say it to you face-to-face."

A few days later, I received a call informing me that company had decided to purchase a similar product elsewhere. My boss recommended I read books on understanding body language so that I could get a better read on people.

I learned that I needed to pay attention when doing business with people. I couldn't afford to be tricked into believing they would help and then have them bail. Carl told me many times that I believed others felt the same as me, even when they didn't.

The impact of my conversation with Mr. Weaver continued to show. Although he was wealthy and powerful—unlike me—he also was a gracious, generous man who wanted to make a difference in Barrow, just as I did. The encouragement he gave me made it easier for me to reach out to those I thought could help. It could have been a CEO or a state political leader and it would not have mattered. I believed in what I was doing and assumed everyone else would too.

It was important for me to communicate well and ask for support. Of course, it isn't always fun asking for money. But because I believed what I was doing would help change lives, I had to evaluate how much that was worth to me. I had already determined it was worth my time and effort. Now I was having to ask myself, *Is it worth doing no matter what people think of me?*

On a trip to one of our kids' games, Carl and I were talking about a friend who was out of a job. I said I would ask one of the dads on the team about giving our friend an interview.

"You ask for so many favors that I bet people hate to see you coming," Carl said.

At first, Carl's words hurt my feelings. Then I started evaluating myself. He was correct; I did ask for a lot of favors. But then I thought of all the people who asked me for favors. I was probably the first person some came to when they needed something, and I enjoyed being asked to help. At the ball field, I not only managed to secure our friend an interview, but I also helped him get a job!

I've been called in professional fund-raising circles "the accidental fund-raiser." I have to agree with the assessment, because many of my original ideas on how to raise money for the Barrow field proved incorrect. I did have enough common sense, however, to understand that I would need buy-in from people who possessed enough resources to make the project succeed. The problem was that I didn't know who those people were because that was not the crowd I hung out in. The most I could do was talk about the project with practically everyone I came in contact with—and that's what I did. I urgently needed a breakthrough. The story of a woman and a group of people from Florida building a field in northern Alaska was interesting, but three months after watching the ESPN story, I needed that interest to transform into money. I needed wise counsel to make that happen, and soon.

HELP FROM ABOVE

One of my good friends from the ball fields, Michelle Spence, had a father known for his success in business. I asked Michelle if she could arrange a meeting with her father, and made clear that I would ask for his advice and not money. I had to ask Michelle her father's name, because Collin and other teammates enjoyed hanging around him when he came to watch his grandson, Michael. The players affectionately referred to him as "Papa Santo."

I respected Mr. DeSanto's business acumen so much that I prepared myself for the possibility he might advise me to abandon the project. After he listened to my proposal and learned why I wanted to put a field in Barrow, he did the complete opposite.

"I get asked for money all the time," he told me. "They are all very worthy causes, but I know the same request will come again next year or even next month. That's because the need cannot be met no matter how much money is poured into it. Your idea is different. It is something tangible—a football field—and has an ending. When the money is raised for the field, you have accomplished your goal. For these reasons, not only will I encourage you to move forward with your endeavor, but I will support it financially and I will present it to others who I know will do the same. I don't think you'll have trouble raising this money."

I realized then and there it wasn't enough to ask people for their support; I needed to be *specific* with what I asked. Mr. DeSanto gave me not only needed encouragement, but also a scenario of how we could raise the money. By the end of our conversation, I was calling him "Papa Santo" too.

Ike Sherlock of the Grimes Companies had been unsuccessful at getting quotes for transportation costs within our quick time frame. In fact, one transportation company had told him that they couldn't provide a quote because, "That cannot be done."

Neither Ike nor I was willing to accept the first "No" as the final answer. Ike was up for the challenge.

"Cathy, I need you to put on that Southern charm," he said, "and I need you to call this number."

I trusted Ike enough to do exactly as he instructed me. "All right," I told him. "I can do that."

I called Bill Deaver, president of Totem Ocean Trailer Express (TOTE), a Seattle-based company that transported products into Alaska. As I walked around my backyard, I started from the beginning about watching the story on ESPN, and how my husband was a coach, and how my boys played football, and so on. I told him about the upcoming press conference and promised that if his company would as little as consider offering their services, I would mention TOTE's name to the media.

"We do a lot of transportation into the state of Alaska," Bill told me. "This is something I think we can do."

We didn't have money to pay for transportation yet, and I wasn't sure if Bill knew I was asking his company to donate its services. So I continued trying to sell Bill. I think this would be considered "overselling."

"We can do advertising. We're going to hold a press conference, and we can make sure that we let people know that your company is a big part of this."

"We're not doing it for that reason," Bill said. Then he shocked me by saying the exact words I had told Carl on that Sunday morning that started me on this mission: "We will do this because that football program is going to save the lives of those young men."

"Yes, it is," I said.

"And that's why we want to be a part of it," Bill added.

A sense of thankfulness overcame me. A businessman—a complete stranger—from the opposite end of the country was completely convinced of the value of this vision to help Barrow. He committed Bill King, his projects and logistics manager, to help us with the project—and that proved to be an invaluable addition to our team. I had struggled to close deals in my sales career, but as I looked around my backyard, it was clearer than before that this project wasn't coming together because of my might or power or skill.

Those coming on board were convinced, same as me, that our work would change lives. My mind revisited the conversation with Kyle the morning he had expressed how embarrassing it would be if the project failed. I recalled what I had told him: "If this is God,

He'll go before us, and He'll tell people to help us. He'll prepare their hearts." That's exactly what God was doing.

Soon after talking with Bill, I was driving to one of Cara's softball tournaments. Judy Adams, a good friend and mother of one of Cara's teammates, was riding with me. Judy was one of the people regularly praying for the project and encouraging me since the early days, and she enjoyed hearing every detail of our progress when we were together. I was updating her on the logistics and told her of the problems caused by the absence of roads into Barrow. The only outside access to Barrow was by water and air, and ice limited access by water to two months out of the year.

"Some of these products are going to have to go by air," I told her, glancing over to her in the passenger seat. "The only thing I can think of that could help, with planes that could do this, would be the military."

"Well, Cathy," Judy said. "My brother is a general in the Air National Guard out of St. Augustine. I'll call him right now."

She called her brother—Brigadier General Joseph Balskus—as I drove. Judy explained the situation and arranged for Carl and me to meet with her brother.

When Carl and I met with General Balskus, we told the story in the same fashion as we had many, many times. The general was enthusiastic about helping, and Carl and I looked at each other in near amazement as he started discussing Air Force bases that could be used and the types of aircraft needed. Then he gave us the names of their specialists to pass along to Ike. Now we had the United States military on our team!

CHAPTER 10

A FAMILY IN
THE MEDIA

The oversized, wooden, farm-style table served as the central hub in our kitchen. The stack of recruiting mail on that table was a daily reminder of how behind we were in processing all the mail addressed to Kyle.

We'd started out keeping Kyle's recruiting letters in a shoebox. That soon needed to be replaced by a bigger box. As the recruiting pitches continued to pour in, that box gave way to just storing them on a closet floor. Kyle received the most mail of anyone in our home. By far. On top of that, each day, he'd come home with a different bundle of mail that had been sent to him at the school. The new arrivals would be placed on the kitchen table to be sorted through. Those from schools Kyle was interested in, we kept. Because of volume, the rest went straight into the trash.

That stack also served as incentive for the field project. As I'd sit at the table and talk on the phone, I'd flip through the mail and envision a day when a Barrow football player's mom would thumb through a similar stack of mail, all from college football programs offering her son the opportunity to receive an education because of the exposure he'd received through Barrow Whalers football.

In late February, about a week before the press conference, I remembered what Kyle had told me about how embarrassing it would be if the project failed. How could I not keep rehearing those words? Although a junior, Kyle had decided which university he wanted to attend. Being recruited to play major college football is a big honor, but a seventeen-year-old is making a decision that sets the course for the rest of his life. The process becomes overwhelming and wearisome, with all the mail, the phone calls, the visits from college coaches, the media interviews, and practically everyone asking daily if he'd made a decision yet. I remembered Carl's senior year of high school, and how awesome I thought it was watching him be recruited. But going through that process with Kyle, as his momma, was beyond stressful.

ESPN.com had ranked Kyle as the number-four quarterback in the nation for his recruiting class and ranked him number thirty-four among all positions. Schools from across the country were recruiting him. The closet floor served as Exhibit A. Yet, during the early stages of his junior season on the baseball team, Kyle had made up his mind that he wanted to attend Clemson.

Kyle had attended a football camp at Clemson after his sophomore year, and the coaches had offered a scholarship on the spot. Kyle loved the campus and especially Dabo Swinney, then the receivers coach and the member of the Clemson staff responsible for recruiting the Jacksonville area. As we came to know Coach Swinney on a personal level, he struck us as an incredible man committed to his faith and his family—one who personified the values we had come to love under Coach Sutherland. Furthermore, Tommy Bowden, a man of high character, was the head coach. It felt like Clemson's program would be a continuation of Kyle's experience at Bartram Trail.

Kyle was also a talented baseball player, with a likelihood of being drafted to play baseball professionally following his senior year of high school. He wanted to play baseball and football in college, and Clemson presented him the opportunity to do both if he accepted a football scholarship.

Kyle isn't one to jump to decisions. He researches thoroughly, and when he makes a decision, he rarely changes his mind. Although numerous other schools had expressed serious interest in him and we expected more scholarship offers, Kyle knew he wanted to go to Clemson. For a highly recruited athlete, making that decision public is usually a beneficial move, because although it doesn't completely shut down the recruiting process, it at least dials it back down to a manageable level. In Kyle's case, he would be able to enjoy the rest of his baseball season and then enter his senior year of high school with that burden removed.

I asked Carl his thoughts about letting Kyle announce his commitment to Clemson ahead of the Barrow project press conference, so Kyle could have that moment to himself. Carl thought aloud about what other quarterbacks might also commit to Clemson over the next year and the possibility of Kyle receiving an offer from a school where he might have a better chance to make a more immediate impact. As we continued talking through the pros and cons, we agreed that as long as Kyle was completely sure of his decision, it would be best for him to make his announcement before the project press conference. The publicity around Project Alaska had been growing. Kyle was already a fixture in the sports sections. We'd heard enough whispers and secondhand accounts of conversations to know the negative side of two people from the same family receiving as much publicity as we were, and we believed that keeping Kyle's news separate from me and the project would be smart.

We called Kyle into our bedroom. He seemed firm in wanting to attend and play at Clemson, and we shared our thoughts on going public with that decision. Kyle called Coach Swinney to inform him that he had chosen Clemson. Coach Swinney was thrilled. After chatting with Kyle, he handed the phone to his sweet wife, Kathleen, and she welcomed Kyle to the Clemson family. Then she asked to speak with me. That phone call affirmed for me that Kyle had made the correct decision and that there was no reason to consider any other programs that would make an offer to Kyle. We bought orange and purple Tigers clothing for the whole family. As Coach Swinney liked to say, we were "all in" with Clemson.

When Carl was being recruited, the recruiting process was much calmer. High school players holding major press conferences to announce their decisions weren't commonplace yet. Carl had made his college choice known at his church, and Kyle thought it would be a nice tribute to his dad to make his commitment known at our church, far from the glare of media lights. Pastor Ron left time at the end of the next Sunday's service for Kyle to reveal he had picked Clemson. Kyle's news hit the papers the next day, two days before the press conference. All the attention was appropriately on him. That proved to be a wise move.

BACKLASH AT HOME

I needed to look professional in front of the media for our Project Alaska press conference, so I went to a local department store to purchase a blazer. As I looked for the right one, I couldn't fight off the thoughts that I was not equipped to handle a press conference. Those thoughts were soon joined by a resurgence of doubts whether I could manage the project to its completion. Then I noticed a friend walking toward me.

"What ya getting?" she asked.

I was so intimidated by the approaching press conference that I didn't want to tell my friend why I needed the blazer.

We scheduled the press conference for Wednesday, February 28, on the Bartram Trail football field—the one the NFL had made pristine for Super Bowl practices. Following Paul's instructions, we set up a rented stage in one of the end zones so we could hang a banner with the project's website name stretching the full width of a goal post.

Paul McCormick had assigned me the task of inviting the partners in the project, and I was joined by my family, representatives from SchenkelShultz Architecture, the Grimes Companies, UPS, ProGrass, the Jacksonville Jaguars, and General Balskus, in addition to all the Bartram football coaches and several players. With the varied industries and interests each represented, they would all bring credibility to our project.

Each of the partners spoke about their enthusiasm for the project despite the unique difficulties. Kyle did a great job speaking on behalf of the team about wanting to help the Barrow players. Xavier Brewer, one of the Thursday night dinner boys who often stayed in our home, and John Watts, another player, also spoke to represent the senior class's buy-in. Kyle, Xavier, and John practiced and played on fields given to them by the NFL, so they could speak to the benefits of the gift their school had received. Coach Sutherland, of course, nailed his time at the microphone by providing perspective concerning the opportunity for our team, school, and community to use football as a platform for serving others. Carl spoke and graciously bragged on me with zeal and support for the project.

The number of media in attendance impressed Dan Edwards from the Jaguars. He confirmed his team's support and stated that although the Jaguars had yet to determine how they would be involved, they wanted the Barrow players and coaches to visit their headquarters when they came to Jacksonville and possibly practice on the Jaguars' practice fields.

With national media in attendance, I wanted to get across that while our area was becoming more involved in Project Alaska, the field also presented opportunities to not only the rest of our state, but also across the country. In addition to the usual story of how I first learned about the Barrow football program, I recounted the phone interview with Barrow's only radio station to emphasize what we held in common with a place so far and so different from Jacksonville: our desire to build great young men.

Then I made a statement that I later learned helped earn me credibility in Barrow: "If we can just change the life of one young man there, then it is worth it."

Immediately following the press conference, NPR and the local ESPN radio station interviewed me one-on-one. Everything at the press conference came off exactly as Paul had planned—it was a huge success.

I don't know if more than a hundred people in the Lower 48 knew about the project before the press conference. That changed overnight when the story hit the Associated Press newswire and went viral, creating the need for us to perform damage control locally.

Coach Sutherland had offered to write a letter of support to go to all parents of our football players ahead of the press conference, because he did not want the parents to assume that we were committing our team and community for the entire $500,000. He wanted to make clear that his program would focus on hosting the kids in families' homes and lending a helping hand to the project where we could. But on the day of the event, I didn't see any parents other than the few I had invited. The news reports of the press conference were highlighted on the local TV news stations as well as in our local newspaper. Most of our players' families learned of our project for the first time from the media—along with the rest of the world. That left many feeling they had been unknowingly committed to a project they knew nothing about. I asked Coach Sutherland if he had invited all the parents to the press conference, and he said he had.

"How did you invite them?" I asked.

He showed me a copy of the letter dated February 20 and said, "I sent one home with every single one of our players."

"Coach," I said, "fifteen- and sixteen-year-old boys don't give their moms notes. Your kids might, but they're in elementary school. Kids in high school don't do that."

Coach Sutherland profusely apologized, and we switched into high gear on developing a plan to address the building criticism. Coach said he could hold a mandatory meeting for parents. Players for the following season would need forms filled out by their parents, and coaches typically held a parent meeting to go over information for the season and establish team expectations. Coach said he could quickly schedule a mandatory meeting to take care of those needs as well as address the project.

MAKING MY PITCH

Ahead of that meeting, I identified key parents I believed would want to take part in the project. I talked individually with them and gained their backing heading into the parents meeting.

I couldn't have imagined going into that meeting without knowing I had a few supportive parents there. I was already sweating bullets before Coach Sutherland started explaining to the parents that he had committed the football program only to hosting the players and coaches from Barrow. He reiterated how the project synced with his program's character development emphasis. Then he allowed me to close the meeting by addressing the parents. This was my first opportunity to share with the other moms and dads my passion for sending a field to Barrow.

My goal was simple: let the parents hear my heart and see how excited I was about the opportunity before us. I described Barrow's social problems, with the school's high dropout rate and the problems with youth depression and suicide. I explained the need for the football program there and the urgent need for a new field. Not once did I talk about the $500,000 we needed to raise. (Kathy Cope later fussed at me about that!)

As I talked, I surveyed the school auditorium to measure the parents' reactions. I had expected some would not buy in. I saw several people with arms crossed, glaring at me as I spoke. A few stood and walked out. I was rambling a little in my excitement, and I'd gone past the announced end time. I couldn't tell who was leaving because of the time and who was leaving because of their opposition. I didn't want anyone to leave; I wanted everyone to embrace the project the same as me. So, watching people exit the auditorium saddened me, but—and this was huge for me because of my people-pleaser personality—I was able to accept the apparent rejections.

My sadness was replaced by elation when I finished speaking. Immediately, a line formed of people wanting to host Barrow players in their homes, wanting to know how they could sign up, and asking if there was any other way they could participate in the project. Because of the enthusiasm of the parents who did come forward, I knew we were going to be fine.

I received no direct negative feedback following the parents meeting; the criticisms I heard came secondhand. Some opposed raising money for a place outside of our community. Even though we lived in an affluent area, our community had its own needs, and much of the concern centered on helping a place far away instead of raising that money for home. When the Super Bowl had come to Jacksonville, the NFL had proposed more at Bartram Trail than upgrading the fields, including constructing a new locker room. The league scaled back its plans amid local concern that Bartram, a new school, would receive things poorer schools in the school district would not.

Just as with the critics in Barrow who contended that money spent on football should be used elsewhere within the school, I understood the perspective of those who favored keeping the money local. But I noticed that those complaining most about what we wanted to do in Barrow were not doing anything to help the needs in our community, either. I disagreed with their criticisms—not with the notion that our area had needs, but the degree to which they compared to Barrow's. Our area was capable of meeting most of its needs itself, and we had grown a little too accustomed to being able to do that. The people of Barrow happily lived off the land, the sea, and the air. They didn't take things for granted like we did sometimes.

A few of our parents, I heard, also had concerns about hosting kids from a challenging social environment like Barrow. They were hesitant to have boys they didn't know from situations they didn't know spend a week in their homes. We had social problems where we lived, too, but ours weren't being talked about negatively in the media like Barrow's.

I had expected pushback and had to accept that I would receive criticism, but the end result would be worth it. I was gradually chipping away at my need to make everyone happy. If we were going to step out and take on a project bigger than ourselves, we would have to leave behind some people who didn't see the good in serving the Barrow team. I didn't want to leave anyone behind, but it's a fact of leadership that when you move forward, not everyone decides to go with you.

CHAPTER 11

UNEXPECTED HELP

South Carolina, Ohio, New York, Washington. We could almost track where accounts of the press conference appeared in newspapers by the states from which the wave of donations came through mail, emails, and phone calls. Reading the notes that accompanied checks provided the most rewarding moments in that phase of the process.

Donations arrived from people with no connections to our area or to Barrow. They had read or heard about the project and felt inspired to help. We received notes from people who had a son who coached, or who had kids and grandkids who played sports. All were eager to do good for others through sports.

One of the more powerful notes came from parents of a young man killed on 9/11. They said their son would have loved to be a part of helping the kids in Barrow, and they sent a $10,000 donation from his estate. A man from Kentucky mailed us a one-dollar bill with a note that said if everyone who heard the story would send a dollar, the field would be paid for. During a baseball game at one of our rival schools, Fleming Island, someone from the school came up to me and told me the school was donating all the admission money for that game to the project. Smaller kids would create their own ways of giving for the field, like placing collection jars at concession stands at their ball fields.

I was still planning on the bulk of the funding coming through a large corporation, or perhaps two. I hoped the press conference would build our case for that sizable donation. But as donations from individuals kept showing up, I accepted that my original plan was not going to happen. Our primary source of donations would likely be individuals, and from many different places. That made the task ahead loom ever larger.

I resolved to make the most of my observation and focus on how we could keep the momentum going with individual donations. I started holding small fund-raisers that various people suggested to me: car washes, golf tournaments, and so on. Kathy Cope helped me understand that I couldn't raise funds this way alone. "You can't have enough golf tournaments and car washes to pay for the field," she told me.

The father of a Bartram Trail player had coached at the professional and college levels. I tapped into his expertise and put together a list of high schools in Florida and along the West Coast—because of its proximity to Alaska—potentially with the resources to assist with the project. Then I did a mass mailout seeking their help. Three schools sent donations. I kept doing interviews with local news stations and also with radio stations across the country. I was invited to speak to sports camps and to groups tied to UPS, and those efforts brought in donations.

I noticed a trend among those who were giving: many stated they'd felt compelled to give because sports had played an important role in their lives and/or their children's lives.

A big donation or two certainly would have made my life easier and required less of my time, but the number of smaller (relatively speaking) contributions that came in pointed back to the unifying power of sports. The way the sources of donations was trending also meant more people would have buy-in on the project, and I liked that aspect. Every donation that came from an individual, whether twenty dollars at a local car wash or a check for a hundred dollars in the mail from a faraway state, would allow that donor to feel that he or she had been a part of helping Barrow—and doing something good in the world. It became important to me that we give as many people as we could an opportunity to belong to the group that would help change lives in Barrow.

And I felt accountable to those who were sending money; I had a responsibility to them to see the project through to completion.

Kathy and her husband, Lafayette, were lifesavers at helping me manage negative emails and phone messages. My nature is to avoid conflict at all cost, but Kathy handled conflict well. Lafayette had corporate experience in human relations and operations, and he could diplomatically respond to criticism with a nice, but clear, email. Like this: "On behalf of Cathy Parker, we would like to thank you for your interest in Project Alaska. Although we appreciate your concerns, we are moving forward with the project and would appreciate your support." And when people told us, in their opinion, what we should be giving the people of Barrow instead of a football field, Kathy replied with her matter-of-fact delivery: "If God has placed that on your heart for the people of Barrow, we encourage you to move forward with it. As for us, we are giving them a football field."

Kathy was perfect for me to align with because the whole process was stretching me, and she was a strong person who showed me that I needed to be bold and not worry so much about what people thought.

Naturally, the criticism grew as the national publicity increased. I remember one call in particular right after the press conference. A woman said her husband had worked in the medical field, and they had lived in Barrow for many years. I was enthusiastic to talk to someone from Barrow who, I thought, would tell me how much she liked our idea and offer encouragement.

"Have you ever been to Barrow?" the woman asked. "You really need to rethink what you are trying to do. You seem like a nice person with good intentions, but you do not know these people. They are lazy, and they drink too much. They don't deserve anything to be given to them, especially a football field."

I had no knowledge of what she claimed. Whether she was correct or not wasn't important to me. I knew from the ESPN story that Barrow faced issues, and I wanted to help. And I knew that whatever issues Barrow was confronting, the discipline and teamwork that come from playing football certainly could help.

"That is exactly why we are giving them a football field," I responded. "The game of football will give them an opportunity to change those things."

Her call provided insight into why someone like me, four thousand miles away and knowing next to nothing about Alaska, had been chosen to deliver a football field to Barrow. I had witnessed the power of football in shaping and molding young men. Especially in my own home. But also, my eyes were open to the goodness in people—ordinary people like me who believed they could help make a difference in someone else's life.

That proved to be an advantage, but I was oblivious to the obstacles ahead.

TEAMING UP WITH A HALL OF FAMER

As our fund-raising efforts picked up steam, it became clear that Project Alaska needed credibility. Although we were receiving strong responses from people when they first heard our story, we lacked a big-name endorsement—that high-profile person willing to lend his or her name to the project. I also hoped we could find someone in Alaska to bring validity to our intentions there.

Both came unexpectedly in Larry Csonka, a Pro Football Hall of Famer who not only possessed national appeal but also had deep ties to Florida and Alaska.

Larry had played running back in the NFL for eleven years, including with the Miami Dolphins from 1968 to 1974 and again in 1979. "Zonk," as he was known, was a member of the Dolphins' 1972 team that won the Super Bowl as the only team in NFL history to go undefeated for an entire season. The next season, the Dolphins again won the championship, with Larry selected as the MVP of Super Bowl VIII. He was inducted into the Pro Football Hall of Fame in 1987. The Jacksonville Jaguars' first season wasn't until 1995, so during Larry's playing days, the Dolphins were the NFL team for all of Florida, and Floridians loved Larry.

Larry remained in the public eye after football through television commercials, celebrity guest appearances on outdoors shows, and by hosting *American Gladiators*. He had moved to Alaska, while also maintaining a home in Florida, and starred in a TV outdoors show called *North to Alaska*, which, at the time, was halfway through a fifteen-year run.

My oldest sibling, Jimmy, had first suggested I call Larry for help because he had come across a story about Larry being involved with the Barrow football program. I looked up an ESPN article on Csonka. In 2004, Larry had filmed an episode of his show in Barrow. While there, he was asked to speak to the Barrow students in exchange for permission to film in and around the town.

Larry shared with the students how much trouble he had gotten into during his school days. On one of his numerous visits to the principal's office, the principal had said that instead of a suspension, he wanted Larry to go out for the football team and take his aggression out on the field instead of in the school hallways.

Because of his name recognition and his understanding of Alaskan culture, Larry connected with the students of Barrow. The student survey that led to the creation of the football program came shortly after Larry's visit.

When my brother said I needed to talk with Larry, I responded, "That's a great idea, but I have no idea how to reach him." Like, yeah, I could just call up a Hall of Famer!

Then one day at work, my cell phone rang with a number from Alaska. I assumed the caller was another reporter wanting an interview. I had decided I wouldn't consent to any more interviews from Alaskan media because of what I considered their negative slant toward me in articles I'd read online. The questions and articles all revolved around the same theme: me not being from Alaska, having never been there, and not really knowing anyone there.

Here I go again, I thought as I looked at the number, *trying to explain my intentions to someone who just wants to write a story about how disconnected I am from people in Alaska.*

The female caller asked if I was Cathy Parker—"The lady working on the field in Barrow."

I gave a "Yes," minus the Southern charm.

"My name is Audrey Bradshaw, and I am the producer and manager for Larry Csonka."

I almost fainted.

"Larry wanted me to call and see if there is anything he can do to help you."

"Oh, yes, yes, yes, yes," I said. "And I'm so sorry that I was short with you. I thought you were a reporter calling."

Audrey described Larry's visit with the Barrow students and how one story he told, in particular, had resonated with them. Larry had grown up without indoor plumbing, she said. (Translation: no bathrooms with running water.) The North Slope still had homes without indoor plumbing, and Larry told the students he could identify with being "the bucket boy." He had the students laughing out loud when he detailed how the principal had given him the option of playing football over a suspension. Larry had followed news reports of the football program starting after he had stirred up excitement for the sport.

Audrey added that she was from Jacksonville and her parents lived in a neighborhood down the street from our home. They had been keeping her updated with everything—and I mean everything—that our community wanted to do for Barrow. I consider it another one of the project's miracles that Larry knew of our involvement and reached out to us to ask if he could help.

I was still in shock, so when Audrey asked how Larry could help, all I knew to ask for was a one- or two-paragraph statement of support that we could add to our website. Larry supplied the following endorsement:

> During my junior high school years I was given the chance of participating in the football program or leaving school for disciplinary reasons. Not only did the football program keep me in school, but it taught me valuable lessons in teamwork, pride, self-discipline, and accomplishment that played key roles in my college and pro careers.
>
> The young men of Barrow have a very rich and unique heritage of teamwork and are appropriately named the Whalers. The addition of a much needed football program in Barrow will positively impact many young men's lives . . . just as it did mine.

Larry wound up giving us much more than the endorsement. He and Audrey sent money for the field and stayed in contact with us. Larry's insight into the Alaskan culture, and Barrow in particular, proved invaluable.

YOU HAVE NOT BECAUSE
YOU ASK NOT

Of all the meetings I was scheduling, strangely enough, the one I thought could prove most problematic was the one asking the commissioner of the Florida High School Athletic Association (FHSAA) permission for Bartram Trail to host the Barrow team during our spring practices.

Coach Sutherland had sought approval from the association a previous year to take our team to Virginia to play a spring game against a team coached by a close friend of his. The teams ran similar systems, and Coach thought the trip and the competition would both be good for his team. The FHSAA denied the request.

The association had a reputation for saying no. I didn't know whether the reputation was well-earned, but Carl told me several times there was no chance the association would approve the Barrow team practicing with ours. Carl had been surprised when Coach Sutherland suggested practicing together. In fact, Coach Sutherland was making plans assuming the Barrow team would watch our team practice and not hold their own practices while here, because that was within the rules and would not require the association's permission. But to me, just watching the practice and not playing didn't fulfill the full purpose of bringing the Barrow team to Florida. Plus, I thought it was such a great idea that I saw no reason why the FHSAA would not agree with me. I was certain they would approve the request.

The FHSAA just so happened to be one of my customers at the mail equipment company, and I was due a trip to Gainesville to check on their account. The day of my visit, I called Coach Sutherland a few times to ask if he could make a call to the association on my behalf, but he was teaching class and I could not reach him. However, he had told me before that he would be thrilled to receive permission for the players to wear cleats and helmets instead of full gear. His biggest hope was for something like a noncontact, 7-on-7 type of passing drills.

I took care of my business with the receptionist at the front desk and asked if I could briefly meet with the commissioner.

"No ma'am," she said. "He's booked up for the next two months."

"It won't be five minutes," I said.

"Nope," she said. "He's booked up for at least two months."

"Well, let me tell you what I want," I said. Then I told her the entire story, from start to finish, and how our coach wanted the Barrow team to come down, stay in our families' homes, and learn from Florida students how to be successful student athletes.

Tears started rolling down the receptionist's face before I even got warmed up.

"Sit down and give me a minute," she said.

I saw the commissioner walk past, and I waved and gave him a sweet smile. He motioned me into his office. Butterflies sprang a surprise attack on my stomach, because I knew this was a one-shot deal.

"You have five minutes," he said.

That might have been the fastest I've told my story. When I finished, the commissioner said, "Mrs. Parker, I have a question for you: has anyone ever told you no?"

"Yes, sir," I answered. "My husband told me not to come here today."

The commissioner snickered. "I'll tell you what," he said. "This is really admirable what you and your team and your coaches are trying to do. You'll get our total support, and I'll give you a letter saying that you can have them come down. But they cannot practice against your team. We would need more time to be able to organize something like that. The teams don't need to be practicing on the field at the same time. It would be fine if your team is helping theirs—that's absolutely fine. But only one team needs to be suited up at a time."

I understood that the association had to make sure that our school didn't receive what could be considered a competitive advantage over other Florida schools by practicing against another team.

"We can handle that," I said.

Coach Sutherland called me after I had returned to my car, and I told him what the commissioner had determined.

"I can't believe that," he said. "That's awesome!"

All Carl could do when I gave him the news was laugh and say in disbelief, "Oh my gosh."

For high school coaches like Coach Sutherland, and Carl, who were all too familiar with the layers of process involved in dealing with state athletic associations, me getting in and out of the commissioner's office in one visit, much less receiving a favorable ruling, could be considered a miracle in itself!

CHAPTER 12

A $40,000 MIRACLE

Vicki Griffis held up the size fourteen pair of flip-flops. The other four friends working in my dining room and I laughed at the sight. Vicki found a way to stuff the flip-flops into the burnt orange backpack designated for the six-foot-eight, 310-pound Whalers lineman who would be staying with her family. We had more than forty such backpacks and shaving kits to fill, one for each of the expected guests from Barrow.

When our assembly line had completed its task, my family dining room looked like a storage room.

The gifts represented the team effort the project had become in the weeks leading up to the Barrow team's visit to Jacksonville. Our community amazed me with its willingness to make the trip a memorable one for the coaches and players.

Under Coach Sutherland's guidance, we had determined that if the people from Barrow would pay for their flights, we would cover all their expenses during their time with us. Our community wanted to *really* take care of our guests.

Determining what to give each guest required research into and consideration of the differences between Barrow and Jacksonville.

Based on average May temperatures, Jacksonville would be about sixty degrees warmer than Barrow. We expected our Barrow friends would not have clothing appropriate for our climate, and when I would say in a media interview or at a Rotary Club meeting that we wanted to provide T-shirts, shorts, caps, flip-flops, and sunglasses for their visit, someone would step forward to provide. On one such occasion, I mentioned that we needed sunscreen. I came home from work that week to find a large box of sunscreen on the front porch.

My list of customers included Colomer USA, a manufacturing plant for J.Crew. On one of my account check-ins there, I was talking about the field project and the upcoming visit and how we needed to find backpacks for clothing and shaving kits for toiletries. "Like these?" one of the women at Colomer asked as she pulled out a backpack and shaving kit. Colomer donated backpacks and shaving kits for the forty-plus people we expected from Barrow.

Restaurants offered free meals for the Barrow coaches and players. Winn-Dixie, a Jacksonville–based supermarket chain, provided flip-flops and sunglasses. Security company ADT donated hats, shirts, and shorts. A church invited both teams to attend a Sunday morning service together.

A group of Bartram parents took on the crucial task of assigning Barrow players to our players' homes. That was a responsibility I did not want by myself, and thankfully Coach Sutherland selected fellow team parents Gary and Laurie Hall and Vicki Griffis to determine the pairings. Our first step was to pray for guidance in matching the perfect host family with each of the Whalers players. Many of the Barrow players had never been outside of northern Alaska, and now they would be traveling four thousand miles to a completely different climate and unfamiliar surroundings.

During my information-gathering process, Trent Blankenship

provided me with detailed descriptions of the players, ranging from what positions they played to their personality types. In addition to Susan Hope, I also talked with head coach Mark Voss and assistant coach Brian Houston to learn as much about the players as possible. I was surprised to hear the roster included one female, Ganinna Pili, a receiver and cornerback.

As I read my notes aloud to the group, the stories of their determination despite hardship moved each of us.

We started with the players we anticipated would be most difficult to place. The first stood six foot four, weighed about three hundred pounds, and had autism. Laurie was a speech pathologist who had worked with autistic children daily, so she picked him and said she would talk to his mother to learn all the nuances that would make his stay comfortable.

Next was a guy named Dave Evikana, a native Iñupiat who had lived in seven different homes over the past few years as he bounced around between family members and foster homes. Consequently, he was reluctant to trust adults. Dave had dropped out of school for a time but had returned when the football program was created. "He's not going to socialize," Trent told me. "Don't take it personally, because that's just the way he is." Dave was also an outdoorsman who loved to hunt and fish. "He doesn't care much for school," I read from my notes. "As soon as the school bell rings, he's off hunting. He comes to school only to play on the football team."

"He sounds just like my son Collin," I said to our parent group, drawing laughter from around the table. I chose our home for Dave.

One player's mother had passed away the previous year, and he lost his father a few days before our meeting. I called Mike and Laurie Parker (no relation), the parents of Andrew from our team. The Parkers' nephew had lived with them and had recently passed away in their home while they were away on a baseball trip. Having wrestled with grief themselves recently, the Parkers were more than willing to welcome this student into their home. "He's the one we want," Mike said. "We'll know exactly how to comfort him."

We worked our way through the names. When outstanding needs or circumstances weren't known, we matched by positions. Carl and I also chose to bring in another player, Cody Romine—a quarterback whom I figured would enjoy watching film and talking about the position with Kyle.

We were intentional about every pairing we made, because we recognized that much of the trip's success or failure would come down to whom we placed with whom.

NOTHING BUT SILENCE

Plans were coming together nicely in Jacksonville, but a major problem on the Barrow end that I was keeping to myself made me wonder whether the trip would actually happen.

I had been talking with Trent or Susan every other day, sometimes daily, to fill them in on the unexpected ways our needs were being met. I was excited. They were excited. But suddenly Trent stopped answering when I called. He wouldn't return calls. Susan seemed to be protecting Trent when I asked why I wasn't hearing from him, saying, "He's not here," or "He's been sick," or "He's at a doctor's appointment." I would practically beg for Trent's cell or home number, and Susan would say she couldn't give it to me.

I needed confirmation that airline tickets had been purchased, and Trent was clearly avoiding me. I got scared, and I was afraid to tell anyone. Even Carl.

Because we lived in a tight-knit community, and because almost all the community had embraced the pending visit, I knew I couldn't let word get out that the trip was potentially in jeopardy. We had become a big story around Jacksonville. The local papers were increasingly covering us and giving us wider exposure, so a reporter discovering I didn't know if the Barrow folks had arranged their travel yet could have been disastrous.

We had received more than $50,000 for the field by that point. We kept detailed records for every donation, but several had come in anonymously. We would have no way to get in touch with those donors and explain what had happened. People and companies had donated items and services for the trip. Transportation companies were well into the process of working out the details for how to deliver the products for the field.

The Barrow football program was the main focus of the project. They had the most to lose if the trip fell through, for sure. But I also thought about what was at stake for Trent and Susan. Trent was the superintendent who had led the effort to start the program. I could envision his career being on the line. From my talks with Susan, I knew how important the football program was for her son, and how much value she placed in him being under the leadership of coaches Mark and Brian because he didn't have a father at home.

As for me, I felt responsible for everything donated to the project, from money to in-kind services to volunteers' time. Kathy had kept good records of donations we'd received online and through the mail. But we couldn't keep track of every gift, like people at baseball and softball games who would pass a twenty-dollar bill to me in the stands (which happened surprisingly often) or would make an anonymous gift through a messenger. Those people were just as invested in the project as those whose donations we could account for, except if things went bad for the project, I wouldn't be able to communicate the problem with them.

Truthfully, I also thought of my personal and professional reputations. If the team did not come to Jacksonville, I knew people would be saying I had lied to them. I panicked as I questioned how well I really knew the people I'd been trusting in Barrow. I'd only talked to them over the phone. I could have formed a false impression. My thoughts turned to, *Have I been tricked? Is this story true? Is this whole thing even real?* Multiple times, I asked God why He would allow me to advance this deep into the project if He knew it would fall apart.

A start-up bank had hired me a month earlier to use my sales background to bring in capital. I knew I'd lose my new job if the project failed. The bank had recruited me for the job because name recognition is important in sales, and our project had generated a ton of publicity with my name attached. With no background in banking, I hadn't felt qualified for the job. I'd been told over and over again, "The most important thing is your credibility." Yet every reason why I received the job offer was on the verge of exploding in front of me if my name became synonymous with a project that raised money for an Alaskan football team that never showed. I was in danger of losing my good name, my credibility, and my job all at once.

I usually called Susan and Trent on my cell phone in my office. But now I was so concerned that a coworker might overhear my pleading with Susan for access to Trent that I would go outside to place calls, even with an ongoing fire in the Everglades that filled our air with smoke when the wind blew from the west.

UNITED IN PRAYER

Numerous times during the life of the project, I believed it was on the verge of failing. Each time, I focused on the people of Barrow. We were investing time and resources. But Barrow residents would be the ones hurt if the football program were to fold, and that thought would motivate me to stay positive and keep working. When I couldn't connect with Trent, though, I grew increasingly anxious that *I* was about to be hurt. That my family would be hurt. That they would be humiliated publicly. This trip was the first deliverable for Project Alaska, and if it didn't happen, my reputation would be ruined. *I should have known better*, I'd think in my lowest moments. *I have deceived a lot of good people.*

I wondered if they were having trouble raising enough money in Barrow, and I called an individual who had been supportive of our preparation for their trip. He owned an airplane, and I asked how many seats he had on his plane. I tried to think of other people who might have a plane we could use.

Those backup plans were based solely on speculation, because I still had not talked with Trent.

I brainstormed who I could call that also knew people in Barrow. One name came to mind: Wayne Drehs, the ESPN reporter responsible for the Sunday morning piece our family had watched. After Wayne heard of the plan for the field, Trent put Wayne in contact with me, and Wayne and I had talked on the phone.

Ten days before the team's expected arrival, I called Wayne and cried as I explained the problem.

"This community has rallied behind what I've said," I told him. "They've believed me. They've given us money, and now I cannot get ahold of anyone from Barrow."

"You're kidding," he said.

I assured him I wasn't.

"Cathy," he said, "I'm very concerned for you."

"What have I done?" I asked.

"Let me try calling," he offered. "They usually answer my call."

Wayne called Trent and scolded him for not returning my calls. Trent admitted to Wayne that the team didn't have enough money to make the trip. Between what the school district was paying and what the players were raising, they were $40,000 short, and Trent didn't have the heart to tell me. Wayne, as the story was recounted, told Trent, "You need to call Cathy and tell her. You don't need to avoid her. That's not the way you handle this. She's wondering if you even exist. You can't do that. It's not fair to her."

Wayne's summary of his conversation with Trent devastated me.

I called my brother Jimmy. He was fifteen years older than me and, because of the age difference, as much like a father figure to me as an older brother. This project had become the closest I had worked with him. With an always-calm voice and impeccable advice, Jimmy was my go-to source for much-needed levelheadedness during the project. But in this conversation, not even Jimmy could be of much help.

A short while later, I called my sisters Mary Ann and Elizabeth. They'd already heard from Jimmy. Unbeknownst to me, Jimmy and Elizabeth were so concerned about the trip falling through and how that could affect me, they called my parents and other siblings to see how much money they could pool together for kids in Barrow who didn't have the money for airfare.

I called Kathy Cope and several other moms on our football team who I knew believed in the power of prayer. They agreed to meet with me that evening and pray for a miracle. Kathy came prepared with notebooks containing specific prayers based in Scripture. We earnestly prayed that God would send money so the team could come to Jacksonville. They encouraged me not to give up—and, boy, was I ready to give up—and reminded me this was God's project and that He would provide.

Susan Hope told me years later that at that same crucial time, she left her office and walked a few doors down to a church, knelt at the altar, and pleaded, "God, please send that money in." People in Barrow and Jacksonville were praying the same prayer at the same time.

Not long after Wayne had called me with the bad news, I finally heard from Trent. Based on what Wayne had told me, I was surprised to hear not an apologetic tone in Trent's voice, but sheer joy.

"We've got another miracle!" he exclaimed.

Then he explained that a father of one of the football players worked for a company based in Anchorage that delivered all the fresh food brought into the North Slope. The father had told the company's owner about the team's trip and how the team was struggling to raise enough money to pay for the travel expenses.

The owner flew into Barrow and handed Trent a check for $40,000—the amount needed to cover all the team's expenses.

Indeed, we did have another miracle to praise God for.

CHAPTER 13

WELCOME TO JACKSONVILLE

That's Brian!

I recognized the assistant coach as soon as I saw him exiting the terminal at the Jacksonville airport. When I had asked Brian for his shirt size ahead of the trip, he'd said, "I'm a big boy—order me that triple XL" in a soft, gentle voice that belied his shirt size.

Carl and I walked toward Brian, and the big ol' teddy bear of a man introduced himself with a bear hug. Brian was arriving a few days ahead of the others, and it seemed fitting that he would be the first face I could put with one of the voices I had spoken with over the phone.

Trent and Susan had told me how well respected Brian was in the school and community, and he'd proved especially helpful in describing the players we would pair with our kids. The details he knew about his players showed he had good relationships with all of them. I had been drawn to Brian over the course of those calls, and on the way to the Jacksonville airport, I'd told Carl, "There's something about Brian—he's really special."

It took just a couple of minutes of talking as the three of us walked the airport corridor and down the stairs to baggage claim for Carl to agree.

Unfortunately, recognizing Brian out of the passengers leaving the terminal proved easier than picking out his extra-large, black suitcase. As the bags started rolling on the baggage carousel, it seemed as though half of the people on Brian's flight had also traveled with a large, black suitcase. Brian grabbed one off the carousel. I didn't see any distinguishing marks on the bag.

"Are you sure that's yours?" I asked.

"Yeah," he said.

We took Brian first to the Halls' home, because Gary and Laurie had moved all the backpacks and shaving kits from my dining room to their house so they could distribute them as each coach and player arrived. Each backpack had been stuffed with clothes and each shaving kit with toiletry items.

"Wow," Brian said when he saw the rows of waiting gifts. "This is for us? These people you've never met?"

A friend who lived near us had moved out of her home for the week to allow the coaches to stay there together. Carl offered to take Brian to the house, and I gave them specific directions on where my friend said she left her key. Carl and Brian couldn't locate the key when they got there, so Carl called me. I explained again where the key should be. When my description didn't match Carl's description of the home, we figured out they were outside the wrong house.

Brian laughed. "Man, I was going to jump in the shower and relax. Just think what they would have thought when they got home and saw a big black man sprawled out on their sofa."

After Carl and Brian found the correct home, Brian discovered that he had indeed picked up the wrong suitcase at the airport. He certainly made a grand entrance into Jacksonville!

FIRST IMPRESSIONS

Fewer than three months after the press conference launching the project, I was welcoming the first of the players to arrive from Barrow and meeting these young men for the first time. While the majority of the team was scheduled to arrive in Atlanta on Friday, May 18, Laurie Hall and I welcomed six of the players early to Jacksonville. After big hugs, introductions, and helping the boys secure their luggage, we made our way outside to load up in our two vehicles and head home. The eye rubbing and yawns revealed the boys' weariness from traveling across four time zones.

"It smells really good here!" one of the boys said, inhaling the lingering smoke from the Everglades fires that had been filling the Jacksonville air for days.

"No, it really doesn't," I said. "That's smoke from the Everglades fire. It doesn't smell good, and I was hoping you wouldn't have to smell that." It hit me that the Everglades needed description. Barrow didn't have trees, brush, or even grass. The people of Barrow couldn't even collect wood to start a fire, unless wood washed up on the beach or was brought in from another area. Most of the time, they had to purchase wood to burn. I did my best to explain the Everglades and how a fire could go for weeks at a time because of all the wood and foliage there to burn.

"It sure is hot here!" another boy exclaimed. Laurie and I laughed to ourselves, thanking God for the overcast skies and unseasonably cool temperatures. What seemed hot to these boys was unusually cool for Jacksonville in mid-May, with highs expected only in the sixties when they could have easily reached into the nineties.

As we made our way home, a storm packing strong winds, heavy rain, lightning, and thunder hit. In our part of Florida, that type of storm might last all of fifteen minutes. This one was big enough that rain pounded my SUV, and I had to turn the windshield wipers to full power as I concentrated on the road ahead. I did take a glance into the rearview mirror to check on the boys in the backseat. Their faces revealed their anxiety.

"Do you guys have thunderstorms like this back home?" I asked.

"One time it thundered, like about five or six years ago," one of the boys answered. "It's so cold in Barrow, we don't get much rain." Later, I learned just how accurate his statement was, as Barrow averaged only five inches of rain in a typical year, despite the forty-plus inches of snow they received per year.

"Wow," one of the boys said. "Does this kind of storm happen often here in Florida?"

"All the time," I told him.

"Is that all coming out of the sky?" another one asked.

"No," one of his teammates said with a laugh. "There's someone on top of the car with a water hose."

I chuckled to myself. This was going to be fun!

A young lady named Amanda Burrell had accompanied the boys on their flights. That night at our house, Amanda, who was a native, talked about the difference in colors she had immediately noted in Jacksonville compared to Barrow, particularly the green of our grass and trees and the blue of the sky after that afternoon's storm had cleared.

"Barrow is just different shades of gray," she said. "The water is a shade of gray, the ground is a shade of gray, and the sky is another shade of gray."

I went to bed that night still trying to process the grayness she had described. I'd never heard of such a lack of color. That was a difference between our two homes that I hadn't anticipated. I wondered what else I would discover.

MAKING FRIENDS QUICKLY

I woke up Friday with a big sense of anticipation. The main travel group would be arriving that evening. I asked Amanda if there was anything in Jacksonville she wanted to see in the time before the rest of the team arrived.

"I'd really like to go to a mall," she said.

Aha—another difference!

I took her to one of the local malls. She wanted to spend so much time there that I arranged for a friend to pick her up while I would be at the school with the arrival party.

The main travel group flew into Atlanta, Georgia, around lunchtime. Three of my siblings lived in Atlanta, and I had arranged for them to meet the rest of the team, minus one player who'd come later, at the airport there. They had food ready for them and ushered them to the charter bus that we had arranged to drive them the final six hours of their journey to Bartram Trail.

Back home in Jacksonville, I eagerly waited for the bus from Atlanta with a growing crowd at the high school that peaked at about two hundred people. Our group held colorful banners, ready to welcome our guests with cheers, as members of the local media sat nearby, poised to point their cameras in the direction of the bus at its first sighting.

Anticipation mounted as the bus's arrival time neared. My heart raced as I thought of all the hours of work by the volunteers who had made this moment happen, and especially as I considered that less than two weeks earlier I had not known if the team would actually make it or not.

When the first group of parents spotted the front of the bus pulling into the school, everybody broke out into loud cheers and chants of "Whalers! Whalers! Whalers!"

Trent was the first to step out of the bus onto the pavement. I walked forward, saying, "Welcome to Jacksonville!" as the two of us hugged. Trent confessed that after all the hours of travel, it was such a relief to finally be in Florida. Meanwhile, player after player filed off the bus, sporting white jerseys with "WHALERS" in big blue letters and each player's number in gold and blue. Armed with brief physical descriptions to help them identify their assigned players for the week, the host parents strained for the first look through the crowd at their guests.

I spotted Cody, the first of the two boys staying with us for the week, right away because he was wearing his number, 2. Cody was a handsome young man with dark hair, even though he was not native. Dave was even easier to spot. He was the last one off the bus, and the only player not wearing a jersey. Dressed in all black, his head hanging low, it was clear that Dave was striving to not make eye contact with anyone.

Breaking through this tough exterior is going to be a real challenge, I thought, as I walked forward to introduce myself to Dave. I was met with the silence Trent had prepared me for. I simply moved on, encouraging Dave and Cody to follow Carl, the kids, and me to our SUV.

We took the team to a group dinner. The restaurant's air conditioning was a new experience for several of the folks from Barrow, because temperatures indoors are kept very warm there. I asked the manager to turn off the air because "our friends from Alaska are really cold." The manager laughed and happily obliged.

Despite the normal awkwardness that was to be expected the first night, by the second day you wouldn't have known that the players belonged to separate teams. It was amazing how quickly they opened up to each other despite their different backgrounds and experiences.

CLEATS AND FURRY SLIPPERS

The first practice was on Monday. Kyle had a driver's license and could drive Collin, Kendal (a freshman on the junior varsity), Dave, and Cody to practice. That day, Cody came out of his room wearing a T-shirt and pair of shorts from the backpacks given to the players—along with furry slippers that appeared to be made from some type of animal. Kyle looked down at Cody's slippers and then, wide-eyed, over to me. "It's okay." I assured Kyle.

Many of our players were driving the Barrow players staying in their homes to practice with them. I noted the pickup trucks pulling into the school parking lot, windows rolled down, arms resting on the open windows, smiles shining as music blared from inside the cabs. Their players were loving life just the same as ours.

In line with FHSAA rules, the two teams didn't practice together. Instead, the Barrow team watched our boys practice, and when it was time for Barrow's players to practice, our boys watched and pitched in to show them skills, drills, and how our team practiced. That ruling proved unexpectedly beneficial early in the week. The Jacksonville Jaguars had committed to providing cleats for the Barrow players. I gathered all the players' shoe sizes for the Jaguars, and we advised the players not to pack cleats for their trip. Unfortunately, the Jaguars decided to present the cleats when both teams visited the Jaguars' practice facility later in the week. In the interim, our boys wound up sharing their cleats with the Barrow players, which thrilled us parents to know our sons were getting a chance to share something they owned with their guests—even if it was sweaty, stinky cleats.

Coach Sutherland ran tightly scheduled practices, with every minute purposely scheduled, and he adhered to the schedule. The Barrow coaches noticed the difference that sticking to the schedule made in the efficiency of practices. Following a scripted, detailed practice schedule would help make the team more competitive when it returned home.

The Barrow players saw firsthand how hard our guys worked when they lifted weights; in many ways, the weight room was an extension of our practice field. The Whalers responded to what they were observing. On the field, even though the teams came from drastically different football backgrounds and levels of expertise, they possessed similar competitive natures and work ethic. The Whalers had won just one game the previous season, but it wasn't because of a lack of effort. Their players clearly wanted to become a good team—they had the potential to become a good team—and they were willing to work hard to accomplish it. The way they lifted weights, it was obvious that even though our boys might be lifting heavier weights, the Barrow players weren't going to be outworked in the weight room. They wanted to impress our boys and our coaches. And they did.

They also had some big boys—the player with the size fourteen flip-flops was one of five linemen who weighed at least three hundred pounds. Our Bartram coaches joked that when it came time for the Barrow team to leave Jacksonville, a few of the larger players they'd like to see wearing a Bartram Trail uniform might "accidentally" miss the bus.

CHAPTER 14

FUN IN THE SUN

The non-football parts of the week were what truly made the visit a success.

The Barrow boys were so nice and polite, and they fit in well. There were two types of players from Barrow. First were the native Iñupiat kids, with their dark hair and distinct facial features highlighted by pronounced cheekbones. The second were the non-natives whose families had moved to Barrow. They were easily distinguishable because of how pale they were—shockingly pale, actually, to us tanned Floridians. As the teams mixed and mingled, and with the Barrow players wearing the clothes we had given them, by the end of the week, sometimes media members were having to ask which teens were from Alaska and which were local.

We parents enjoyed sharing the individual experiences from hosting the boys. Many of the stories involved food. Those boys could sure eat! Midweek, Laurie Hall told me the groceries she had bought for the week were already gone. Knowing that orange juice and milk were expensive in Barrow—milk cost over eight dollars a gallon there—she had made sure her guests would have plenty. Yet, neither lasted long. Laurie laughed as she told me how for the first breakfast, she wanted to fill up the two players from Barrow and her son, so she cooked an enormous breakfast that included a dozen eggs, a pound of bacon, and a large stack of pancakes. The three boys made quick work of those and remained at the table, looking for more to eat.

Laurie had fruit at the ready.

"Do you get grapes in Barrow?" she asked.

"We get them for our mom for her birthday," one said. "She keeps them in the freezer as a special treat, just for her."

"Well, you definitely can have as many grapes as you want," Laurie told them. She walked to the refrigerator and opened the door.

"Do you want red or green?" she asked.

One of the boys responded, "They come in different colors?" Who would have thought grapes could offer a lesson in the differences between our parts of the world?

Cody, Dave, and our boys went over to the Halls' home. The boys were knocking around a ball in the swimming pool, and one of them hit the ball out of the pool and onto the lawn. A Barrow boy jumped out of the pool and ran to retrieve the ball. When he stepped onto the grass, he immediately froze in his tracks.

The concern was that he had seen a snake or stepped into a mound of fire ants.

"I've never felt grass before!" he exclaimed.

GATOR BY THE TAIL

In planning the week's activities, we knew the trip would not be complete without letting the folks from Barrow see a real, live alligator. None of our Bartram Trail players could relate to the subsistence living in Barrow, but they did at least feel they could brag about how big the gators, deer, and other wildlife grew in Florida.

Our family liked to eat at Outback Crab Shack, a family-owned restaurant that had a dock along the St. John's River that had to be the length of five football fields. In preparing for the week, Kyle and I had visited with one of the owners, Joe, and explained how we wanted to bring the Barrow team to eat there and take them out onto the dock so they could look around at the surroundings. Joe showed us the menu, which included many seafood options, but he recommended chicken for such a large group.

"I'd really like for the Barrow folks to try something that we're known for here in Florida, something that would be new and unique to them," I explained to Joe.

"How about gator tail?" Joe asked.

"That would be perfect!"

Joe offered more. "There is a big gator back there that has been a nuisance," he said, "and I will have the warden come out and bring it up here for those boys to see. We'll let them pet it."

Kyle's eyes got really big!

People who grew up in the marshes of Florida thought nothing of not only catching an alligator but also *petting* one—snout taped shut, of course. Kyle and I were excited and nervous about introducing our Barrow guests to a new Florida friend.

The day of the teams' visit to the restaurant, the owners invited Coach Sutherland to help bring the captured gator to the restaurant. Coach was originally from Ohio, so he didn't grow up catching gators in marshes. But he was game for an adventure.

When the owners and Coach pulled up to the restaurant with the gator in their pickup, the Barrow players weren't the only ones whose jaws dropped. Even our boys were taken aback to see a gator so massive that its tail was hanging out the back of the truck. The snout was securely shut with duct tape, but as that big ol' monster snorted, few from either team were brave enough to pet it. And although only a handful returned to Alaska able to boast—truthfully, anyway—about petting an alligator, all the coaches and players sampled gator tail. Their consensus: it tasted like chicken.

JAGUARS, THE BEACH, AND CHEERLEADERS

The week also included a baseball game and barbecue at Jacksonville University and sightseeing at the Fountain of Youth and on a trolley tour in St. Augustine. The highlight for most seemed to be the visit to the Jacksonville Jaguars' facilities to watch the Jaguars practice, followed by a lunch for both teams plus Jaguars head coach Jack Del Rio and many of his players. Carl couldn't recall a better meal during his time in the NFL. The Jaguars presented the Barrow players with black Reebok cleats.

Cody, the Whalers' quarterback, had a particularly enjoyable day. Maurice Williams, a Jaguars offensive lineman, engaged in a lengthy conversation with Cody about the trip. Then Cody sat at a table with Jaguars quarterback Byron Leftwich, who signed Cody's shirt and chatted with him for a few minutes. The Barrow team was able to practice on the Jaguars' practice field, next to the team's stadium, which had hosted a Super Bowl two years earlier. Brian Houston said the day was beyond anything he could have expected.

Wayne Weaver, the Jaguars' owner, took time to shake hands with the players and coaches. He called me after the team left and said that the Barrow team made such a positive impression on him that he would write a personal check for Project Alaska.

A day at Mickler's Beach for both teams also was part of the sched- uled activities. My kids always accused me of being an overprotective mother, and I hadn't been convinced the beach was a good idea because I didn't know how many of the Barrow players could swim. The thought of seventy-five teenage boys horse-playing in the Atlantic Ocean made me nervous. For the most part, we had avoided any serious issues during the trip. The exceptions were a couple of players who encountered problems from exposure to the sun. The worst was Dane Enoch, one of two players who stayed with Gary and Laurie Hall. Dane started suffering from migraine-like headaches because of the sun, and an optometrist prescribed sun-darkening glasses that the Halls purchased for him. Despite the lack of problems, it still was fortunate for me—and more fortunate for the players—that I was unable to accompany the teams to the beach. I wasn't there worrying about the boys, and they didn't have to put up with me saying, "Don't do that!"

A few Bartram Trail cheerleaders happened to show up at the same part of the beach, much to the delight of the Barrow players. Terry Brown, a reporter and photographer with the *St. Augustine Record*, had met the teams there to interview players and take pictures. The front page of the next morning's paper featured a photo of one of the Barrow players, Addison Cox, jumping to catch a football alongside three of our bikini-clad cheerleaders. Addison and the cheerleaders were all smiling.

The picture thrilled me, because Addison was the player whose father had passed away a few days before the trip. The folks in Barrow had doubted that Addison would come to Jacksonville. Seeing the picture of Addison having fun—the youthful joy on his face—made me realize that every second of the work setting up the trip was worthwhile. I couldn't wait to show Addison his picture in the paper. When I did, his response surprised me: "Oh, no. This is not good."

"Addison, making the front page of the newspaper is a good thing," I said.

"Not when you have a girlfriend back home," he said.

I laughed. "Oh, Addison, she'll never know. She won't see it."

The next day, I looked at Alaska newspapers online. One had run that exact picture.

Oh, yeah, I thought. *He's done.*

My family on the Bartram Trail High School football field in Jacksonville.

The Bartram Trail team at our press conference.

Me with the Bartram Trail football team seniors.

The Barrow Whalers arriving in Jacksonville.

Carl speaking about Project Alaska Turf.

The Barrow Whalers getting used to a warm Florida welcome.

Right: Bartram Trail and Barrow Whalers visit a St. Augustine Alligator Farm.

Below: Whalers' Robert Vigo joins the Lawrence twins.

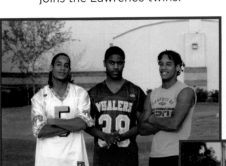

Bartram Trail players helping the Whalers practice.

Barrow Whalers' Albert Gerke learns some fundamentals.

Barrow players take a knee to thank me and Bartram Trail High School.

The Barrow Whalers enjoyed seeing the Jacksonville Jaguars practice.

Whalers' Van Edwardsen receives an autograph from a Jacksonville Jaguar.

Whalers' Coach Mark Voss talks with Jaguars' Coach Jack DelRio and Bartram Trail Coach Darrell Sutherland.

Kathy Cope and I going up to see an aerial view of the field.

Many thanks to the companies that delivered the field products to Barrow!

The Barrow players pitched in to make sure their field was ready for the season-opening game.

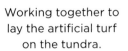

Working together to lay the artificial turf on the tundra.

"Woman Power"— Miss Pili in action.

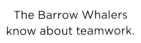

The Barrow Whalers know about teamwork.

It was a joy to have my daughter, Cara, with me in Barrow.

Coming together from opposite corners of the United States, Susan Hope and I share about family, faith, and football.

God stamped the Top of the World with a blue-and-gold football field to show His love for these people.

Photo courtesy of the late John Gleason: his picture shows how atypical football is in the arctic.

Some of our Florida group with young Barrow native Joseph as their tour guide.

First time on the turf—
touchdown for me,
too cold for Cara.

Youth from surrounding
villages travel to Barrow
to learn to play football.

NFL legend Larry Csonka
speaking with the Barrow
Whalers before kickoff.

Everyone was excited
and cheering at the
Whalers' first game
on their new field.

Taking time to thank
God for all this team
had experienced.

Upper Left: Doing the coin toss is harder than you might think.

Left: I've watched a lot of football games in my life, but this one was special!

Above: It has been a privilege to do something that blessed an entire community.

Cheering when the Barrow Whalers scored the game-winning touchdown!

We celebrated as we witnessed another miracle in the form of a win!

Upper Left: They are proud to be called the Barrow Whalers.

Left: Bill, Ike, Tom, Brad, and Scott celebrate by a bone from a bowhead whale.

Above: Carl and Coach Brian Houston talk football during our 2018 visit.

They don't pour Gatorade on the coach in Barrow; they jump into the Arctic Ocean after a win!

Judy Adams and I experienced the exhilarating polar plunge.

CHAPTER 15

A LIFE-CHANGING WEEK

I had been naive about Barrow.

It was a remote town of about forty-six hundred. Saying it had limited access would be an understatement. I had wrongly pictured a somewhat controlled environment because of the absence of roads into and out of Barrow.

During the team's week with us, I was surprised to learn that many of the social problems a big city like Jacksonville faced also were prevalent in Barrow. I listened to heartbreaking stories of widespread abuse of alcohol and drugs such as marijuana, cocaine, and methamphetamines. Too many youths lived in homes without their fathers. In those ways, Barrow was no different from where we lived.

Several of the Barrow boys described how boredom contributed to the number of youths who got into trouble, admitting that even for themselves it was a game, of sorts, to do something that would result in the police being called. There weren't enough good options for the time the young people had on their hands.

But football was helping. It not only provided something to do, but it produced the positive by-products of discipline, accountability, and purpose. The community had loved coming to the games in the first season, and the players responded to that support. They wanted to be a good team; they didn't want to continue losing. They wanted to give their community the gift of a winning football team. I started seeing why Coach Sutherland had wanted the team to come to Florida and stay in our homes—so they could see what a student athlete's life looked like. Our coaches and players could help the Barrow players accomplish their goal.

The Whalers' week in Jacksonville increased my awareness of how important the field would be to helping the football program survive, and how important the football program was to the youth of Barrow.

THE COACHING COMMUNITY

The trip turned out different for the Barrow coaches than they had expected. They had scouted our area online and made plans to visit places they wanted to see. A greyhound racetrack down the road from our house and a few restaurants had caught their attention during their research. But once they got a taste of Coach Sutherland's character curriculum, they scrapped all their plans for independent sightseeing so they could talk more football and character development with our coaches.

The coaching fraternity is interesting. Few people outside of coaching circles understand the pressures and demands on coaches. The hours are long and pull coaches away from their families. Coaches are competitive by nature and hate losing; they expect to win games, to have winning seasons, to win championships. But at any given game, only one of the two teams playing can win. In high school sports, parents of one of those teams will go home unhappy. The pressure on coaches to win is immense. And by the way, a coach is expected to win while doing things the "right way," as subjective as that may be.

Because of all those factors, the high school coaching community is tight-knit. There's a level of cooperation that would surprise those who haven't coached or lived in a coach's home. High school coaches understand the pressures and demands that come with each other's jobs, and they help each other. Now, consider the extraordinary circumstances that brought the Barrow and Bartram Trail coaching staffs together, and it's easy to imagine an especially deep bond developing between the coaching staffs.

The last night of the visit, Carl and Coach Voss talked for hours in our driveway. I was curious about what they could talk about for so long. I didn't want to go out and interrupt them, but I kept glancing out the window. Several times, I could see both were emotional.

Carl told me that Coach Voss had said the coaches thought they were coming to Jacksonville to learn the X's and O's of football, but that they had learned much more. Carl said he and Coach Voss cried as they talked about the same opportunities they had in very different circumstances to impact young men for the rest of their lives.

Carl developed a kinship with the coaches that has lasted far beyond that one week. I heard stories from parents of similar relationships developing between their sons and the Barrow players in their homes.

BREAKTHROUGH

My biggest regret is that I didn't savor more of the time with our guests in our home—Cody, Dave, and Amanda. I can get so busy with responsibilities that I wind up looking back on events and wishing I had enjoyed them more. Carl and our kids took up my slack and gave good care to our guests. But the moments I was able to enjoy make me wish I'd slowed down more to fully witness and just be present.

Cody and Kyle, the two quarterbacks, really hit it off. Cody was a good athlete and one of the few Whalers who had played football previously. That experience was one reason he was playing quarterback. Cody told us how disappointed he had been when he had moved to Barrow with his mother, because he assumed that his football-playing days had ended. Living in Barrow had been difficult for Cody because he'd moved from a larger area with plenty of sports and activities to keep his calendar filled. Barrow didn't even have a movie theater, he said. But the birth of the program had given him another chance to play football and something to do with his time.

Many of the Barrow players brought gifts for their host parents. We had barely introduced ourselves to Cody when he gave me a framed picture of a polar bear and a carving of a polar bear. While Dave didn't give us a gift, we thought nothing of it, especially given what we knew of him and the tough exterior he wore.

When we took Cody and Dave to our house, Cody was curious to discover what his backpack and shaving kit contained, so he took all the clothes and products out and neatly lined them up on the dresser. Dave didn't open his backpack.

The first night, I noticed that Dave slept with his bedroom light on—I presumed because he didn't trust us. Or adults in general, really.

But Dave's transformation that week still brings tears to my eyes. My son Collin played a significant role in creating the opportunity for that to happen, starting with the first evening, when Dave and Cody rode with us from the school to the group meal.

I knew Collin especially would be eager to launch into conversation with Dave, being that Collin is a people person to the max and was so looking forward to having a fellow outdoorsman staying with us. He had even taken down the mounted bass from his bedroom wall, explaining, "They catch whale. I'm not going to have an eight-pound bass up on the wall that I was proud of when I was five." And sure enough, the second we closed the doors on our SUV, Collin started in with questions for Dave about hunting and fishing—what kind of boat Dave had, what kind of equipment he used, and so on. Dave responded politely but quickly, seemingly eager to end the conversation, if it could be considered that. But his lack of talkativeness didn't deter Collin one bit, and Collin kept the questions flowing until we reached our destination.

Collin "forcing" Dave to answer questions on that first car ride appeared to have softened Dave up ever so slightly. That proved important, because Collin connected with Dave during the week. Our house backed up to woods that led to the St. John's River. After practices, Collin and Dave would come home and head out to explore the woods and river. They were clearly enjoying each other's company and their shared interests in the outdoors.

As Dave opened up, he almost seemed to feel sorry for us because of where we lived. He talked enthusiastically about how fortunate he was to live in a place like Barrow, where he could hunt whale and caribou. He wanted us to come to Barrow so he could show off his community to us.

"We're going to get you that field, and then I'll come in for a game," I assured him. "You just need to stay in school and do well."

"I will," he promised.

One day Collin asked me in front of Dave, "If we do well in school, can Dave come back? Can I go out there to Barrow?"

Dave listened keenly, clearly in favor of the idea.

"Yeah, if you both make As and Bs," I said. Collin wasn't a great student, largely because he didn't care much for school. Both boys could stand to work toward such an academic goal.

Dave and Collin left the room and came back a few minutes later with a counterproposal.

"What about Cs and Ds?" Dave asked.

I conceded to Bs and Cs.

Underneath his tough exterior, Dave had a fun sense of humor that came out more and more throughout the week. Larry Csonka had donated a six-day, seven-night hunting and finishing trip to the Aleutian Islands, with proceeds going toward the turf project. The

Safari Club International North Florida Chapter had a big fund-raiser scheduled the weekend the Barrow team was in town, and the chapter allowed us to auction off the trip with Csonka. I arranged for a few Barrow players to attend on behalf of their team. I thought that as a hunter, Dave would enjoy going, so I took him and Collin.

I got lost on the way to the event. I knew I was supposed to be going west, but I couldn't figure out which direction was west. After a few aggravating minutes of trying to gain my sense of direction, I pointed and asked the boys, "Is that west?"

Neither knew.

"I thought you were a big outdoorsman," I said to Dave. "You don't know if the sun sets in the east or the west?"

He shot back through a wry grin, "The sun doesn't set where I'm from."

Touché!

Both teams were at a park one day, and a large number of media members were there. I was shocked to see Dave answering reporters' questions, and one of the adults from Barrow said they had never seen Dave talking like that, much less with complete strangers.

I asked Dave what the reporters had been asking him.

"You know, just talking about Collin and how we have so much in common," he said.

He delivered his answer nonchalantly, as if talking to reporters were nothing new to him. But it was truly a big deal seeing how far he'd come from his exit off the bus just days earlier.

The day before the Barrow team left, I was alone in the kitchen. Dave walked in with a sweet smile on his precious face and handed me a wrapped gift that he had apparently kept secretly in his room. With Dave watching, I opened the present: a necklace and a polar bear made of ivory.

I reached out to give Dave a big ol' hug, and he hugged me tight in return.

It occurred to me: if we could see this change in Dave in just one week, how much more would the teenage boys of Barrow change over time, through the years, as a result of football? Dave represented the countless more teenage boys in Barrow whose lives we could help change through the field. He loved his Iñupiat culture, but he needed help too. Football was bringing that help, and I knew there were more like Dave in Barrow—then and to come as the football program aged.

If we could just get them a field, we could give them an even stronger foundation for their football program to build upon for years to come. The field would stand as a reminder that even though Barrow was in one of the most remote parts of the United States, people from across the nation had sacrificed and shared their resources for the youth of Barrow. I believed that football field could help Barrow feel less isolated, less alone.

BRIAN'S BIG DECISION

A number of Bartram players attended Fruit Cove Baptist Church, and their pastor invited the teams and host families to attend their Sunday morning service. I became overwhelmed with emotion as I looked around the church at all the people connected to the trip under one roof, worshiping together. I may have cried the whole service, just thinking about the way God had orchestrated this project and brought all of us together here.

Barrow's Coach Brian had kept quiet about not wanting to attend the service, secretly determining he wouldn't attend. Yet when Sunday came, he tagged along anyway, angry because he felt expected to attend, even though this was never a requirement. I later learned that Brian belonged to a faith that prohibited him from attending a place of worship in the Christian faith.

Brian chose to sit in the back of the sanctuary. He later said that was his way of rebelling against being there. Brian gradually moved closer to the front as the service progressed. Something was stirring inside of him.

Following the sermon and when the crowd had been dismissed, Brian walked up to the front to meet the pastor.

"Can I get baptized here?" Brian asked.

The pastor informed Brian that a baptismal service was planned for that evening and that he could return and be baptized.

Mike Parker called me that night to tell me the great news. "This has nothing to do with football," Mike told me. "This has nothing to do with a football field. God's got a different plan."

Mike was correct; the football field was merely a tool for the greater work God wanted to perform in the lives of the Barrow team, as well as the Bartram team. God truly had a different plan—a much bigger plan.

A few months later, Kathy Cope was able to discover Brian's backstory. When Brian was young, his grandmother had taught him about the Lord and that the Lord loved him. When Brian grew older, he chose to follow a different faith. Before the trip to Jacksonville, he had been contemplating what his grandmother had taught him, and he recognized how far he had moved away from the Lord. Brian said he was so far away that he did not know how he could return to what he had believed as a youngster. The key moment for Brian came after Carl and I picked him up at the airport and he saw all the stuffed backpacks lined up at the Halls' home.

"When I saw how you all loved us," Brian recalled, "I was like, 'This is how I get back.' I knew what I had to do when I was down there, because I knew that was where God's love was."

BACK HOME AND BACK TO WORK

For Friday morning, the final day of the visit, we invited the community to take part in a fund-raiser pancake breakfast at Applebee's.

We almost packed out the restaurant, and I took a few moments to watch the Barrow players walking around, introducing themselves, and shaking hands with members of the community who had come to donate to the field. I wished their family members back home could have been there to see how respectful the players were and how at ease they were interacting with strangers. Again, I was struck by the difference in the players' confidence from when they had first stepped off the bus into, for them, the uncertain world of Jacksonville. I felt like a proud momma!

The big farewell took place at Bartram. As sad as I was to see our friends from Barrow leave, I was also concerned with how our rising temperatures might have affected the players had they stayed longer. The team would be moving on to football camps in other states while they were still in the Lower 48—a schedule that Carl said our players, who were accustomed to the warmer climate, would have struggled with.

Host families hugged the players who had stayed with them. Phone numbers and email addresses were exchanged.

As during the rest of the week, my time was mostly occupied with making sure all the logistics for the team's departure came through. But I did suspend my busyness long enough to get Dave and Cody together. I gave them both big hugs and stepped back so I could look them in their eyes.

"I'm going to be praying for you," I told them. "You're forever in my heart."

I wasn't the only one who felt that way.

The team's visit made a significant impression in our area. Even before we left the school to return to our homes, parents were thanking me for allowing them to host the players. To this day, I have not heard one negative story from a host family.

And Carl—oh, my. I'd seen the change taking place in him during the week, especially in his talks with the coaches. Carl had been mostly lukewarm to the field idea, but after the team left Jacksonville, he told me he was feeling a pull in his heart toward northern Alaska.

"What would you think about moving to Barrow so I could coach there?" he asked me.

I loved his intentions, but our family couldn't realistically make that move. But hearing Carl's full-on support on the heels of getting to know the players and coaches had me raring to get to work on delivering what I had promised them: a new field.

The relationships built during that visit increased the urgency to get the field funded. The stakes felt higher now—seeing the impact that the past week had made in these players' lives, and imagining how much greater difference the field would make.

From various conversations with the coaches from Barrow, I learned that opposing coaches were saying they wouldn't play in Barrow that upcoming season because of safety concerns. The cost to play all away games would have been more fodder for the program's opponents. Project Alaska could not use "next year" as a fallback plan. If the field wasn't installed for the upcoming season, there likely wouldn't be a football program the following year. There might not be a season that fall without a new field. The pressure to complete the project had ratcheted up a notch.

PICNICS ON A BLUE FIELD?

The following week, Steve Coleman from ProGrass called.

"What do you think about going with blue turf?" Steve asked. "It's Barrow's color."

I'm a traditionalist when it comes to football fields, and I hadn't been a fan of the trend of making artificial turf fields any color other than green. Okay, I'll say it: I considered nongreen fields ridiculous. Grass is green—if you're going to make an artificial field that simulates grass, it should at least be green! Plus, I had pictured a green field in Barrow since the beginning, because on the land void of grass, green would have stood out.

Steve said the end zones and logo at midfield could be yellow. He gave me an unconvincing list of reasons blue turf would be good, including speculation that blue might hold heat better.

"Steve," I asked, "is blue cheaper?"

"Yeah. And it's already available."

"Okay," I conceded, concerned the blue turf would look fake.

I mailed a one-by-one-foot sample of blue turf in a Plexiglas case to Barrow and waited anxiously for feedback.

Somewhat to my surprise, the feedback came in the form of enthusiastic approval of making the field in their school colors. One person told me townspeople were looking at the sample turf and remarking that they couldn't wait to go out on their new field and have a picnic.

I had to think about that statement. I'd heard the term *tundra*, but I didn't understand the ramifications of living on a frozen tundra, like Barrow. Hearing the story about the player who stepped on grass for the first time in the Halls' backyard had opened my eyes to the reality that the people of Barrow could never go outside and sit on plush grass, and that what seemed like a simple picnic to us in Florida was impossible in Barrow.

We had raised about $150,000 of the $500,000 we believed we needed to transport the field to Barrow and have it installed. The team's visit had provided a boost to our efforts in Jacksonville, and I was hearing enthusiastic reports from Barrow that the turf would be perfect for them.

But after the team returned to Barrow, Trent's enthusiasm from the trip diminished with each phone call as he described the growing opposition to football. Trent sounded like the fan of a football team whose opponent was, first down by first down, steadily marching downfield for a late, game-winning touchdown. The game hadn't been lost yet, but a negative outcome seemed inevitable.

"Cathy, I don't know if we're going to even have a program," he told me on one call.

I tried to encourage Trent by letting him know that everything involving transportation of the field remained on schedule, and how once we got the field to Barrow, the support would be there. Fulfilling our mission took on even greater significance.

But then I received a call that put the entire project in jeopardy.

CHAPTER 16

CRITICAL STATE

From his first involvement with the Barrow project, Ike Sherlock had been the can-do guy for much of the logistics in delivering the Whalers' new football field to a place unreachable by roads. We had talked less than an hour earlier, with Ike jovially giving me the date the last barge would leave Seattle, Washington, for Alaska before Arctic ice would block off the destination.

The tone changed for this conversation.

Right before calling Ike, I had ended my call with the representative from the company producing the field. Ike had asked me to inform the turf company of the barge's departure date. The turf company rep replied with, "Well, Cathy, you know . . . I've got some bad news for you."

The publicity surrounding our effort to replace the Whalers' field had caught the attention of executives with the turf company, and they didn't like hearing that we still were raising money. Now, with less than two weeks until the last barge of the year to Barrow left Seattle, I was being told that the pallets of rubber mulch—one of the field's three components—being shipped out of Canada would not be released until we paid the full amount.

We didn't have the money yet. And we wouldn't have the money in time. I explained to the rep how donations were still coming in at a good rate and that because no one had attempted to send a field to a place like Barrow, we could not anticipate the total cost.

"I'm sorry," was the best he could offer.

So, I called Ike back with the turf company's stipulations—either the full amount paid or a guarantor, plus a list of signed documents.

"What other options do we have?" I asked.

"There are none," Ike said.

I couldn't find a single word to say. I had to have other options, because the Barrow football team had no other options. If the Whalers did not have a new field by the start of the season in August, their program would not survive.

I felt the entire weight of the field on my shoulders. If in the beginning I had known how impossible this project was, how the program's very existence would depend solely upon completing the impossible, I would not have made such promises.

The field *had* to make that barge.

"If it's not on this barge, it's dead," Ike continued. "The whole project's dead. It cannot happen. There are no other ways we can get these products in time."

Then he delivered the disheartening blow: "Cathy, in my professional opinion—and I've been doing this for years—we need to either delay or terminate this project and let people know as soon as possible not to expect a field for this upcoming season."

Tears flowed before I set down the phone. Carl had stood next to me in the kitchen, listening to my end of the conversation. He knew the turf company's stipulations and my inability to meet their demands. Carl reached out to embrace me. I buried my face in his shoulder. This was the moment, I realized, when Carl could finally tell me, "I told you so."

My obsession with supplying a field for Barrow had, at times, burdened Carl and our four kids. I'd worked countless hours on top of my full-time job. I'd brought extra, often unwanted, attention to a family already in the limelight because of athletics. There had been times when my family had wished I would just let it go. But I couldn't.

As I sobbed into his shoulder, Carl held me, 100 percent supportive of me. But there was nothing he could do either.

"You've done the best you can," he tenderly told me. "You had the team here. You made a huge impact. It's not your fault. At some point, you have to realize you've done all you can do, and that this was an impossible project. There are some things we don't have control over and we can't do. It's okay. It's okay to say you gave your best effort."

I agreed. I hoped that people would see that I had done my best, that I hadn't tried to scam them. But I had to admit that the project had outgrown my capabilities. I had taken on a task I could not complete.

I spent the rest of that night quiet and broken. I couldn't call my closest friends and tell them the project was over; I'd have to wait until the next morning to do that. I started formulating a public statement in my mind, because I'd need to contact all the media who had covered us and let them know. And I needed to tell my new friends in Barrow. I couldn't imagine how crushed they would be to know there would be no field and, thus, no more football. They deserved to know right away, but that call would wait until tomorrow too. I didn't have the strength to tell them yet.

I went to bed that night angry with God because I *knew* He had given me this assignment. Unable to sleep, I prayed—and my prayer was not one of thanksgiving. It was direct, and it was raw.

God, why would You have me do something when You knew it couldn't be done? Why would You do that? Why would You do that to me and make me look like a fool?

Emotionally exhausted, I finally fell asleep for a few hours.

I woke up that morning more resolute than ever.

God had given me that vision, and where He gives vision He also gives the faith to see the work through. It didn't matter to me that everyone else who knew what was going on believed the end had come. I knew we could finish this project. I knew God would provide the way. I just didn't know how it would happen. For the first time during the project, my response to a hurdle that popped up in front of me was not self-doubt, but a resolve to continue working until we accomplished our goal. Until that field was in Barrow and the football program was alive and the team was playing games on it.

I had talked with Kathy Cope the night before, and she set up a time of prayer for that morning with our prayer team. Only Kathy knew of the *other* problem.

UNYIELDING FAITH

I had believed much of the opposition existed because of misperceptions about the field itself. Knowledge came second- and thirdhand. I would have loved the opportunity to communicate directly with the opponents and clear up the misperceptions. But I didn't know who the opponents were—until a week earlier, when the phone call came from a group opposing the project.

It was whaling season, and a number of natives who supported football were out whale hunting. During the supporters' absence, the opponents had gathered residents for an informal yes/no vote on the field. The naysayers won. We were two months from the start of the season in mid-August and the deadline for installing the turf, and they called to inform me the people had voted not to allow the field to be placed at the planned location. Furthermore, they warned, if I proceeded with the project, they would pursue legal action.

This group had previously claimed that the field would be too difficult to maintain. Supporters in Barrow had tried to explain that because the field was artificial turf, maintenance would be much easier compared to their current field. Now the group was telling me there was no place to store the field when it was rolled up following football season. I explained that the field would not need to be rolled up, because it would be a permanent fixture with an expected life span of at least ten years, but I didn't seem to be making any progress with them. The opponents also continued to argue that the field would be a waste of money.

I could only hope that once the group saw the installed field, they would understand why we wanted to give it to them and be grateful to have it. But with deal-breaking land *and* transportation issues, the project was in serious trouble.

While Kathy and the prayer team gathered, I called Scott Barr in Barrow. Scott was a chaperone who had accompanied his son and the team to Jacksonville, and I had come to know Scott fairly well during the trip. He proved to be a trusted advocate for the football program. With supporters of the project out hunting, I hoped Scott could help me. I told him about the turf and land issues.

"I've got to have some help there," I told him.

"Give me a little bit of time," he said. "Let me gather some people."

While Scott went to work in Barrow, I drove to the SchenkelShultz firm to meet with Brad Hill. When Brad had committed SchenkelShultz's help at that first Rotary speaking engagement, he and Jim Stege, the managing partner, went all in with us. Brad, with his arctic architecture knowledge, had worked with ProGrass to communicate the needs for installing a field on the permafrost.

Brad and Jim were both delighted to see me walk in, because

they enjoyed hearing regular updates on all phases of the project. I requested to speak with Brad in a conference room, because I wanted to ask what documents were needed to install a field. I detailed the previous night's conversations with Ike and the turf company, hoping he would suggest other ideas for obtaining the products we needed to install the field.

I didn't tell Brad about the land being unavailable. I figured that for this meeting, the transportation issues constituted a big enough problem on their own. One disaster at a time, right?

"I still believe it can be done," I told Brad. "We've just got to talk to the right people."

My hope made no sense on the surface. I understood that as I expressed it. But I still had hope.

Brad was emotionally attached to the project because he had spent hours on the phone lending his expertise to the suppliers and talking with the Barrow coaches about the ground and the field. Our families had become friends through the process.

"Cathy, this is a great idea," he said sympathetically. "But you've got to understand that these types of projects take three to five years. This isn't a project that gets done in a few months. These things take years."

"We don't have years," I told him. "That field's got to go in or they won't have a season."

Brad asked Jim to join us in the conference room and updated him. Perhaps Brad thought that if they outnumbered me, I would understand that getting a football field installed in Barrow by football season was impossible.

Brad and Jim invited me to sit at the conference table.

"Do you have a permit for this field?" Jim asked.

"No," I answered.

He wrote *Permit* on a bright-yellow sticky note and placed it on the conference room table.

"Do you have a deed for the land where this field is going?" he continued.

"No."

He wrote *Deed* on a pink sticky note and placed it on the table.

Jim went through a long list of questions. Each time I answered with "No," he placed another sticky note on the long, mahogany table. At the end of his questions, the table was filled with multiple colors of bright sticky notes that represented needs that must be met before construction could begin.

I didn't care.

I had enormous respect for Brad's and Jim's abilities. Their conference room wall was lined with renderings of beautiful buildings they had planned and seen through to fruition. I appreciated their concern, and that they cared about me and the project. Everything they were saying was correct. I knew that in the natural, there were steps of progress that needed to be followed. *This*, *this*, and *this* would have to happen before *that* could happen. Brad and Jim knew every box that needed to be checked. Except I wasn't working off of knowledge; I was working off of faith. I had gone through all the emotions of the previous night after my phone call with Ike and then awakened to unyielding faith. God had given me that vision and the faith to see the project through to the end. I understood what Brad and Jim were trying to persuade me of, and I knew they wouldn't understand what I had to say. The conversation had grown uncomfortable for me, and I couldn't see any improvement soon. Conflict-avoidant to my core and recognizing my ongoing need for their input and help, I needed to end our conversation politely and respectfully.

"I know this looks bad," I interrupted. "But I am telling you that if we can talk to the right people in Barrow, we can pull this off."

The looks on Brad's and Jim's faces screamed, *Poor Cathy—she doesn't get this*.

"Could I just have a moment to dial in a friend in Barrow who's helping me reach the right people there and move this project along?" I asked.

Brad and Jim nodded and left the room. I took a deep breath as I dialed Scott Barr's number, praying he'd pick up.

FAITH TO BELIEVE

"I've got the elders together," Scott reported. "We'll be calling you in a few minutes."

I stepped out into the hallway of SchenkelShultz Architecture to ask Brad the number to the conference room. I passed it along to Scott and brought Brad and Jim back into the room. Scott was driving across town, I told them. In Barrow, that requires only a few minutes.

"They've assembled the community elders," I said. "They can help us."

Scott called from the conference room of Ukpeaġvik Iñupiat Corporation, or UIC, an Alaska Native corporation with headquarters in Barrow. UIC provided social and economic resources to Iñupiat shareholders and their descendants. The company was dedicated to preserving the Iñupiats' heritage. (Ukpeaġvik comes from one of the Inupiaq names for Utqiaġvik, Barrow's native name, which means "place to hunt snowy owls." In 2017, residents voted to change the city's name from Barrow back to Utqiaġvik.)

Scott had managed to bring together six elders who were among the most respected men in their community. Jim took charge of the meeting. "Okay, why don't we just start with everybody introducing yourselves, telling us your titles and your contact information? Do you guys have email?"

"No, we're in the Stone Age," one of the natives sarcastically responded.

Oh my gosh, I thought. *This is off to a bad start.*

I whispered to Jim, "Let me do the talking."

The men from the UIC board room introduced themselves and began to explain who the Iñupiat were and their culture. Pride radiated through their voices as they described for us the importance of the whale to their community, and how they harvest and distribute the whale to feed the community, including which portions are used and for what.

The elders took their time in describing their customs and heritage. Eventually, Brad and Jim both were called away to meet with clients but indicated they could return if their expertise was needed. Alone in the SchenkelShultz conference room, I sat fascinated as I listened to the elders.

When it was my turn, I talked about our pleasure in hosting the Barrow team. "Your young men were so polite and honoring," I said. "They won over the hearts of the people in Jacksonville. Barrow should be so proud of them."

I shared that the social problems in Barrow I'd learned of were common to us in Jacksonville, too, and that we also had young men living in broken homes or enticed by alcohol and drugs.

"My husband coaches high school football, and my boys play high school football," I continued. "My husband and the coaching staff have had opportunities to mentor these young men through football. It's not just about the game; it's not just about winning and losing. It's an opportunity to see these lives changed. Football has impacted our family and our community in so many positive ways. I don't know if football will change your young men for the better, but it has ours. If you are willing, we would love to help your community by giving it an artificial turf field, like the fields our youth play on."

There was brief silence.

"Now is the time," one of the elders said.

Other elders, one by one around the room, repeated that phrase: "Now is the time."

Goose bumps raced up my arms.

"There are some things I need to tell you," I said.

I detailed the phone call from the group of opponents that had told me about the vote to not allow the football field where we had planned. "So we don't have anywhere to put the field."

The men laughed. One told me, "The UIC owns *thousands* of acres of land."

"The turf company refuses to release the products unless we pay all of the money up front or have someone who can sign a guarantee that all of the bills will be paid." I said. "I feel like we'll have the money by then, but we have to have somebody who will guarantee it."

I took a deep breath, reluctant to admit what needed to be said next: "We're at a critical state."

The men talked among themselves in their native language, and my mind raced, anxiously wondering whether I'd said too much. Finally, one of the men addressed me.

"We have sat back and watched our young people go in a direction that they shouldn't," he said. "And it's time that we step up. We will give you the land to put the field on. We will give you a foreman to oversee the work, and all of our equipment will be at his access to be able to put the field in."

"I need to ask you one more thing," I said. "What about the contract and the money?"

"We'll sign the contract," replied the man, whom I later learned was the UIC president, Anthony Edwardsen. "And if you don't raise the funds, we'll sign that. We will guarantee it."

I felt the need to make sure they understood what they were agreeing to sign.

"We are still raising money, and our hope is that we'll get the money we need," I explained. "But we might not, and the turf company is going to expect their money."

"If you're not able to come up with the money," the president said, "we will guarantee it."

Tears formed in my eyes. The last obstacle I could see had been removed. *Thank You, God*, I prayed.

"Thank you so much," I told the men.

I hurried to find Brad and Jim and told them the good news.

Brad hugged me. Jim said nothing; he just stood there, stunned.

"Looks like we're putting the field in!" Brad said to Jim.

MANY WHEELS TURNING

I faxed a contract for the turf payment to UIC. It took a few days, but the elders stood by their commitment and had it signed and returned. When I received the contract, I called Ike so he could start the trucks carrying the mulch to Seattle, from where the barge would leave in three days.

"Cathy, this is not the way you do transportation," Ike told me. "You always leave a few days' leeway. What if there's a flat tire? In transportation, you have to plan for those situations."

I laughed, because with all that God had done to get us to this point, I wasn't going to waste a second worrying about a flat tire.

"There's not going to be a flat tire," I said. "You have no idea what all is going on. Just call them and tell them to get on the road. It's going to be fine."

Indeed, it was fine. The rubber mulch arrived in Seattle in time to make it onto the barge of Bowhead Transport Company, a Seattle-based subsidiary of UIC that shipped into the Arctic Slope of Alaska. The Bowhead barge left Seattle for Barrow on June 30.

The main part of the turf was being made in Chatsworth, Georgia. The inlays—the non-blue parts of the field that would be sewn into the main turf, such as the white yard lines and numbers, yellow end zones, and yellow Whalers logo for midfield—were still being manufactured at ProGrass's headquarters in Pittsburgh, Pennsylvania.

Those products, the final two, could be shipped later by air, because they weren't as heavy as the pallets of rubber mulch.

To provide a sense of the complexity of the transportation logistics, plus the number of transportation companies that partnered with us, here is an overview of how the turf, inlays, and installation tools made it to Alaska:

- UPS provided the local trucking and trailers to take two loads of the main turf ninety miles from Chatsworth to Norfolk Southern Railway in Atlanta. (I showed anyone who I thought would be remotely interested pictures of the turf-carrying semis being placed on rail cars.) UPS also supplied trucking and trailers to carry two loads containing the inlays and all the installation tools from ProGrass's Pittsburgh headquarters to Norfolk Southern Railway in Pittsburgh.

- Norfolk Southern took those loads from Atlanta and Pittsburgh to meet up with Burlington Northern Santa Fe Railroad in Chicago, Illinois. BNSF carried the four trailers to Seattle, where UPS took over delivering the loads to TOTE's terminal in Tacoma, Washington. The two trailers containing the turf arrived at TOTE during the day on July 12. Trailer number three, with the installation tools, made it that night. The fourth trailer, with the inlays, arrived the next day.

- A TOTE barge carrying three of the four loads left July 13 and arrived in Anchorage four days later. Those loads were then trucked to Fairbanks. The fourth and final load left Tacoma on July 20, with a scheduled arrival of July 24. That load would then be transported to join the other field products in Fairbanks.

I had learned to expect the unexpected, but I hoped that we had cleared our final major obstacle.

Of course, it couldn't be that easy.

CHAPTER 17

BLACK MONDAY

On Monday, July 23—our "Black Monday," as it would become known—Ike called me at my office while he was on a family vacation and told me, "I need you to get on this conference call—now."

I closed my office door and dialed in using the number he gave me, joining a conference call concerning the Air National Guard's role in flying the inlays into Barrow. People representing four time zones were on the line, and there were attorneys on the call. That was a sure indicator that we had a serious problem. The Air National Guard had figured out a way to use one of its training expeditions to fly the field products on C-130s from Fairbanks to Barrow. But one of the attorneys on the call informed us the Alaska Air National Guard would not be able to help after all.

"This is not a military mission," the attorney said, "and we can't be a part of it."

I walked out of my office and down the hallway to the elevators. I looked to see that no one was in the hallway. I leaned my head against the wall and said, "God, I don't know how we're going to get through this. This obstacle is bigger than any I had anticipated. I don't think I can I take any more. This is so hard. And it's falling through again."

I thought of the Israelites from the Bible. Like them, I had experienced one miracle after another that I knew had come from God, but then when I found myself in the middle of the next trial, I didn't think I could continue. No matter what God had done for the project, it didn't seem to be enough for me to carry on.

Ike and I started scrambling, rereading every email we'd received from the Air National Guard, trying to determine what we had misunderstood. We learned later that the publicity the project had garnered had worked against us, making the mission one that created concern for the Alaskan Air National Guard because of its nonmilitary nature.

With previous issues—and there had been plenty—I'd made only a tight circle of people aware of what we were facing. This time was different. This time, I was desperate and didn't care how many people knew. We needed all the help we could get to solve this problem. We needed a miracle. I wanted everyone who knew how to pray to be praying. Kathy sent a detailed email to a long list of recipients, asking for prayer. "Unless there's a miracle," Kathy wrote, "the field won't happen." She and her prayer team set a time to assemble once again.

Kathy sensed my weariness.

"You can't give up now," she told me.

I racked my brain trying to come up with a solution, and Bill King of TOTE started trying to put together contingency plans. Collin's best friend, Tyler Froeba, came to my mind. Tyler, who was sixteen, had served as a page for U.S. Representative John Mica from our congressional district. I thought if I could talk with one of our politicians, he might be able to persuade the Alaska Air National Guard to change its mind.

I filled Tyler in on our situation. He contacted Representative Mica's office to see if any help was available there. The congressman's office, along with General Balskus, connected us with the National Defense Transportation Association (NDTA), a nonpolitical, nonprofit organization that brings the private sector in to aid with philanthropic and humanitarian missions.

The NDTA jumped in right away, and within a few days, Alaska companies Sourdough Express and Carlile Transportation Systems became the eleventh and twelfth transportation companies working with us to deliver all the field components to Barrow. Both volunteered to work together to truck the materials from Fairbanks to Deadhorse (Prudhoe Bay).

One company said it would drive the materials to a certain point and then hand them off to the other.

"These are competing transportation companies," Ike told me. "I've never seen anything like this."

One of the truckers on the call from Alaska spoke with a Southern accent. "I'm from Alabama," he told me. It eased my spirit to have a Southerner involved. "I'll drive through the night if I need to," he assured me.

DEAD END IN DEADHORSE

Deadhorse, Alaska, describes itself as being "at the end of the earth." Good luck finding a place that could contest that claim. Or would want to. Like Barrow, Deadhorse sits at the edge of the Arctic Ocean. It is four hundred-plus miles due north of Fairbanks, to the southeast of Barrow. If you've seen the reality TV series *Ice Road Truckers*, you may remember truckers driving Dalton Highway. That highway ends at Deadhorse, an unincorporated community with a population below fifty. The only people you'll find there are oil workers of Prudhoe Bay and adventurous tourists. Deadhorse also has been featured on *America's Toughest Jobs* and the BBC's *World's Most Dangerous Roads*.

Deadhorse was the end of the road for the turf products and tools. Literally. But they were still two hundred miles from Barrow.

Northern Air Cargo—our *thirteenth* transportation company—offered to fly the inlays on its Boeing 737–200 planes from Prudhoe Bay to Barrow.

The last leg was accounted for. God had provided a way yet again.

The field installers arrived in Barrow on July 25, allowing them a full day of rest before the scheduled installation start on Friday, July 27. The installation tools and three rolls of turf arrived at 10 p.m. on the 26th. More rolls of turf, including all the inlays, came the following day. The rubber mulch arrived on the 28th, and the final pieces of the field made it on Wednesday, August 1. The scheduled date of the first game on the new field: August 17.

Typical installation of a field requires forty-five to sixty days. If there was one thing we had working in our favor—and it had to be the only thing—it was that Barrow had twenty-two hours of daylight at that point of the year.

I received daily photos of the progress by email. A few showed football players carrying rolls of turf after practice. UIC, as it had pledged, provided all the equipment and machinery we needed.

Getting the field installed in time for the first game required a community effort, and much of Barrow turned out to help. As work on the field sped along, I didn't hear anything from those in Barrow who had opposed the project. I assumed that meant some of them had changed their minds.

A DIFFERENT KIND OF INSTALLATION

As the first turf field above the Arctic Circle, installation had to go differently than elsewhere.

Modern artificial-surface fields include underground drainage systems that drastically reduce the number of rainouts and delays teams must endure. With Barrow's permafrost, there was no chance of putting anything underground. Houses are built on stilts there. The Whalers' field had to be built up from the ground using telephone timbers because concrete would have been too expensive.

Installers discovered the glue that holds the field and the inlays together wouldn't work in Barrow's cold temperatures. Brad Hill, back in Jacksonville with his arctic architecture expertise, helped navigate this and other issues as they arose by phone.

Delbert Rexford, the on-site foreman in Barrow, pulled twenty-hour days. This kind man, who oversaw logistics for UIC, had no construction experience, yet he'd been eager to take on the challenge UIC had given him. But as soon as word of Delbert's role got out in Barrow, I started receiving emails criticizing the choice. I trusted UIC and politely responded to each complaint by noting that UIC had provided Delbert to us and confidently stated that he was who we would work with. Delbert responded by handling his responsibilities like a man on a mission.

The first time I talked with Delbert on the phone, I told him how all the markings on this field would be permanent. "No one will have to go line the field with flour anymore," I said.

"Good," Delbert replied, "because the birds keep taking away the flour."

Once the installation began, if my phone rang with a call from Barrow, Delbert more than likely was the caller. I was grateful for his updates on everything, despite having a little trouble understanding his thick accent, although he was fluent in both English and Inupiaq. I can only assume he had difficulty understanding my Southern accent too.

I think Delbert felt empowered by being appointed foreman. He knew the land there, and he wasn't afraid to tell the turf company when their ways wouldn't work there given the uniqueness of the location.

Delbert knew the land better than he knew football. His lack of football knowledge would make me laugh at times, like when he proudly informed me that the installers were making so much progress that they were already to the "75-yard line."

He called once to report a ripple on the northwest end of the field. The top of the permafrost freezes and thaws, causing the ground to shift. The ground could not be completely leveled. I tried to picture the ripple's location on the field until I figured out it was in one of the end zones.

"I'm not going to worry about that," I said. "Once the players get into the end zone, they won't care one bit about that little ripple."

CHAPTER 18

WARM RECEPTION

O nly God brings people to Barrow."
Tavia Barr, Scott's wife and a parent of one of the Barrow players, had told me that once on a phone call. A Jacksonville-area supporter donated money specifically so thirteen of us could make the trip to Barrow to experience the first football game on the new field. My trip to Barrow opened my eyes to the truth in Tavia's statement. I gained a new perspective regarding the distance between Jacksonville and Barrow.

I'll put it this way: from Jacksonville, Seattle is barely halfway there. No flights connected through Barrow; it was the end point of all journeys. Once a plane landed in Barrow, the only direction it would go was back to where it came from.

Tavia and Susan Hope were my unofficial consultants in preparation for the trip. Carl and I had lived in Ohio when he played for the Cincinnati Bengals, and his career took me throughout the North. Even though I had experienced more cold weather than any Southern gal would want, I anticipated the North Slope would introduce me to a whole new level of cold.

I asked Tavia what type of clothing I needed to bring. She recommended layers much thicker than anything in my closet.

"Are you sure I need that in August?" I asked. Temperatures in Jacksonville at the time were topping a hundred degrees. "Are you sure it's going to be that cold?"

"This is our warmer time of the year," she said. "But it can get pretty cold, especially with the breeze coming off of the water. Just make sure you have several pairs of wool socks."

"Wool socks? I don't have any wool socks."

Tavia laughed.

Thankfully, we had neighbors who had moved in from the North, and they loaned me the winter clothes they still owned. I had a difficult time trying to imagine what the weather would be like and just how cold it could get. And if I thought I had a sense of what the flights would be like from prior coast-to-coast trips when Carl and I lived in California, I was wrong. I underestimated how grueling the flights to Barrow would be.

But the biggest unknown—and the one that most concerned me—was what to expect from the people in Barrow.

Our Jacksonville community's enthusiasm for the trip was high. We still had a few detractors, but the public criticism had reduced to a faint level after it became clear the project had drawn enough supporters to continue moving forward. The giving end of the project brimmed with positivity. It was from the receiving end—Barrow—that I didn't know what to expect. I knew that because of the compressed timeline caused by the transportation problems, the community was pitching in to help meet the deadline. But there still were enough hurtful emails—like the one that accused me of exploiting Barrow for my fame—and the persistent complaint that the field was a waste of money, to make me nervous about the trip.

Despite my nerves, I eagerly anticipated seeing that beautiful blue field in person, putting faces to names I had come to know by phone and email, getting a firsthand look at the Iñupiat customs that fascinated me, and most of all, cheering on the Whalers players and coaches we'd come to love as they ran onto a safe home field for the first time.

BEAUTIFUL IN BLUE

Carl and our boys were unable to go to Barrow because of their football obligations at home. Thankfully, Cara was able to travel with me, and our group consisted of Brad Hill from SchenkelShultz; Tom Gloe from UPS; Ike Sherlock from the Grimes Companies and his wife, Jen; Kathy Cope; Vicki Griffis; Bartram Trail football players Kyle Griffis and Evan Hall; Bartram Trail High School principal Brennan Asplen; and Judy Adams, one of our prayer team members. We also hired and paid for the trip of freelance reporter/photographer Terry Brown so he could document the trip for the media back home.

Boarding the flight out of Fairbanks, I noticed faces I recognized from TV, and then during the flight, word filtered to us in the back of the plane that those people were from ABC News. The pilot came over the loudspeaker and said, "If I can have your attention, I want to announce some special passengers we have today." I thought it was cool that he would introduce the ABC News crew, because obviously, if they were on this flight, they had to be covering the game. The pilot continued, "Cathy Parker and her friends from Jacksonville, Florida, are on this flight." The passengers turned around to see us and applauded.

That announcement and the presence of ABC News on our flight told me that the opening of the field was an even bigger story than I had expected.

Flying into Fairbanks, I was surprised to see the mountainous terrain and how green the ground was. On this leg of the trip, our flight passed over more beautiful mountain ranges before crossing over into the Arctic Circle. As we neared Barrow, the cracks and crevices of the tundra gave the appearance of dried-up marshland. We flew over vast, flat terrain lacking vegetation or signs of people. Tavia's words rang in my ears: "Only God brings people to Barrow."

Dozens of small lakes dotted the landscape on our descent into Barrow's Wiley Post–Will Rogers Memorial Airport. I looked for the football field as our plane descended, but was unable to spot it, even though I expected its blue and yellow colors to stand out. The town appeared to be confined to one area of tightly aligned rectangles of streets surrounding a handful of bodies of water.

We touched down in Barrow around 6 p.m. on the Tuesday before Friday's game, more than thirteen hours after we had left Jacksonville— and that's with gaining four hours' time crossing the time zones. Outside the terminal, rows of people cheering and waving and holding hand-made signs stood along the chain link fence. Our group walked over to the fence to return the greetings. An elderly lady reached out to me, saying, "I prayed that God would send you. And God sent you." Others around her were calling out my name as I tried to connect voices with names I'd become familiar with through phone calls and emails.

PRIORITY DESTINATION

Even though we were worn-out from the flights, we asked our hosts if we could drive directly to the field—we couldn't wait any longer to see it. The field was about five miles northeast of the airport. The streets and playgrounds we passed along the way were muddy, and I recalled the anticipation of having picnics on the field. The whole town needed this field.

The installation crew, plus the Barrow townspeople helping as a newly trained installation crew, were working hard as we pulled up to the orange construction fence surrounding it. On one side, a retention lake came so close to the field that there was not room to put any seating for fans on that side. I laughed to myself, wondering how many crazy throws or kicks of the football would land in that lake someday. Across the other side of the field, where bleacher seating had been placed, the Arctic Ocean was a hundred yards from the sideline. I'd heard of the field sitting next to the water, but surveying the field in person for the first time brought to reality the idea of building a football field right next to the *Arctic* Ocean.

I had received photos of the field in progress, but oh my goodness! It looked so much more amazing in person. I got out of the car and started walking toward the field. A hopper sat in one corner of the field, because spreading the mulch into the turf still needed to be completed. The press box was still under construction. Seeing what remained to be finished was a relief, because I knew those tasks could be finished by Friday.

I made my way toward the middle of the field, marveling with every step through the cold wind whipping off the ocean at what it took to bring that turf to Barrow. We'd chosen to place the school's traditional logo at midfield in yellow—whale hunters in a sealskin boat, with a bowhead whale breaking through the surface of the water. I'd been concerned over how well the turf company could reproduce the logo because of its intricate details, but it appeared perfect. I stopped on that logo—blue inside in a yellow circle about fifteen yards wide—and looked all around me. I couldn't believe the turf was actually in place. And that I was finally standing on the field. At that point, I was completely confident we would raise the money we still needed. All we needed was pictures of the completed field to convey to others what we were experiencing.

The next day, the ABC News crew asked Kathy and me to fly over the field with them in a helicopter. From the air, we were able to fully comprehend the vastness and how desolate the land was around the field. I had been told Barrow was a land of gray, lacking distinct colors, and I had noticed on our first look around town that the only color appeared on man-made objects. Because of the lack of natural tones, anything that could be spray-painted stood out. Signs were printed in bright hues. The city's emblems were ornate. Even dumpsters were brightly painted.

The aerial view accentuated the grayness of Barrow. The ground was gray, the sky was gray, and the water was gray. I had a difficult time discerning where each began and ended—they blended as though they were one. From the air, I couldn't believe how bright the field's colors appeared. The Whalers' blue and yellow field burst through the surrounding gray. A blue field had been the correct decision.

As I soaked in the view from above, I could not imagine anyone who would argue the field was not beautiful. But more than the color the field brought to the landscape, I thought about the beauty that the field would help bring to the community—and prayed that it would prove a useful home for a sport that could change the lives of its players, coaches, and fans for years to come.

That evening, when I emailed Carl and the boys back home, I couldn't find words to portray how stunning the field appeared from the air. "The only way I can describe it is that it looks like God stamped the top of the world with a hundred yards of the most beautiful blue and yellow I have ever seen," I told them. "It just stands out. And it's a symbol of God's love for these people."

BUSINESS WITH PLEASURE

The people of Barrow welcomed our group with VIP treatment. Of course, we stood out as visitors in the small town, and it seemed as though just about everywhere our group went, a momma or a daddy or an aunt, uncle, or grandparent stopped us so they could thank us for the field. Many did so with moist eyes. They showered us with gifts, too, that reflected the people's pride in where they lived.

Barrow had few accommodations then. Part of our group stayed in the hotel, and others were hosted in homes. Kyle Griffis and Evan Hall, the two Bartram players, stayed in players' homes, and they were able to play a game of touch football with Whalers players on the field. Cara and I stayed in an apartment above a doctor's office—with the thermostat set on eighty degrees when we walked in. That alone qualified as a warm welcome! The accommodations they set up for all of us were comfortable and thoughtful, and meant so much to us.

Daily events created a building anticipation of Friday night's game. At one gathering, I showed players a video that EA Sports had made specifically for them. That summer, Kyle had taken part in the Elite 11, a prestigious national quarterback competition in California that EA Sports sponsored. I put together an information packet for Kyle to take with him, and he presented the field project as an opportunity for EA Sports. I received a message from the CEO pledging a $20,000 donation and a special video encouraging the players and wishing them good luck for their season. Being video game–playing teenagers, they loved the video, although they seemed slightly confused as to why the president of EA Sports would send a message to them. I could tell it hadn't registered with them yet that they were becoming a big deal. They had no idea how much support they had from all parts of our country.

Alaska Airlines hosted a reception for us. Arctic Slope Regional Corporation, a large family of companies with a corporate office in Barrow, hosted something like a community-wide cookout, with grilled hamburgers and hot dogs. The event was *outside*—after all, with temperatures in the forties, the weather was great for a cookout by Barrow standards. As I had been warned, the wind coming off the ocean made the temperature feel much cooler.

Vicki, with teeth chattering, joked to me, "The next time you get a vision, would you make sure there are palm trees in it?"

I envied Tom Gloe and Ike Sherlock, because with the field delivered, their work was done. They enjoyed a stress-free three days leading up to the game.

Funds still needed to be raised to finish paying for the field, so Kathy Cope and I squeezed appointments into our busy schedule. The trip needed to serve a dual purpose as a business venture along with the celebration. Kathy stayed by my side the entire time, driving me to appointments, keeping me on schedule, and setting up any last-minute meetings that arose. I placed Cara, Kyle Griffis, and Evan in charge of sending emails each day to media back home that reported on our trip.

The people of Barrow loved Cara. She's adventurous, so she fit right in. I asked Judy Adams to look after Cara because of my schedule. After we returned to Florida, I found out a native man had invited Cara and Judy to go hunting. Another day, Cara was standing with some of our group at the edge of the ocean when two natives pulled their old boat up to the shore. When the men offered to take anyone interested out to hunt seals, Cara jumped right into their boat. The men spotted a seal and followed it out into the Arctic. The native guide with our group got concerned that the seal hunters were getting out too far and fired a rifle into the air several times to signal them to come back. Cara thought nothing of how far out they had ventured; she was too disappointed that they were so close to getting a seal and had to stop their pursuit.

I was thrilled for the chance to have dinner with Dave one evening where he lived with an uncle and aunt, Nathaniel and Ida Olemaun, who graciously hosted us. His uncle was the mayor of Barrow. After we ate, Dave and his cousins showed a video of them whaling, their eyes lighting up and their speech quick as they explained what we were watching.

"That is really cool," I said. "When you are going whaling again?"
Dave smiled. "As soon as you leave."

The brightness of Dave's face told me why he loved Barrow so much and felt sorry for us city folks and our limited opportunities for hunting and fishing.

Of course, our group had to sample caribou meat and muktuk—whale blubber and skin, eaten boiled or pickled. Barrow residents loved muktuk. Even the kids who turned up their noses at eating vegetables would pile large portions of muktuk on their plates. Our group's consensus: it tasted okay, but we wouldn't want to eat it every day. Most of us slipped our remaining muktuk onto Evan's plate, because he would eat it all rather than risk hurting anyone's feelings.

I knew a trip to Barrow would not be complete without partaking in the tourist ritual of joining the Polar Bear Club by jumping into the Arctic Ocean and fully submerging. The authenticator for entry into the club agreed to send each of us who dove in an official certificate that included the temperature of the water at the time of entry. The water was twenty-eight degrees for our plunge. I had only *thought* the cookout by the Arctic Ocean was cold. My strategy was to take the plunge and quickly run back to shore. Except when show time came, my legs wouldn't move as fast as my mind was telling them to.

The people of Barrow were so kind to us, and we enjoyed getting to know them. Any fears I'd had about our reception were quickly abated by our warm welcome.

IÑUPIAT VALUES ON DISPLAY

The diversity of faith in Barrow surprised me, with different types of churches that I was told were well attended. I knew Susan Hope was a Christian, and I had heard that many Barrow residents had been praying for their community and their youth for a long time, going back well before the school started playing football. Being in Barrow and experiencing how strongly connected the natives' faith and culture were, though, especially in regard to whaling, gave me so much more context to understand how isolated Barrow was and how dependent the people were upon nature. It made sense that their beliefs were so closely tied to what God provided them through nature.

Many residents believed that God provided the whale and that the whale knew whether the people were worthy of its giving itself up to them. The locals explained that a whale had the ability to dive deep into the ocean and flee, but if it deemed the captain and crew deserving, it would come to the surface, where it could be harpooned.

To make this belief more plausible, the eardrum of a captured whale was placed on the mantel in the captain's home so the whale could hear how the captain talked to his wife and his children. The captain had to display to that eardrum his worthiness of the whale sacrificing itself to be captured. After touring the Iñupiat Heritage Center and seeing how small a sealskin boat was, and that it could hold only three or four men, I had to agree that a man capturing this massive creature in such a small boat had to be a true act of sacrifice on the whale's part.

The tour guide at the center explained that each member of a whaling crew had a specific job, and if each job was not performed with excellence, not only could that spoil an opportunity to catch a whale, but it could also cost the crew members their lives. Seamstresses were considered part of a crew, and each one stood at the same position of a boat every time she sewed the bearded skins over the sparse frame of the boat. That way, if the stitches came undone on a hunt, it could be determined which seamstress was responsible for the loss of life.

The devotion with which the natives held the Iñupiat cultural values was evident throughout our visit. Their values were intentionally woven through every element of the culture. Although not linked directly to Scripture, biblical principles were evident in the list:

- Respect for Nature
- Family and Kinship
- Avoidance of Conflict
- Cooperation
- Humility
- Hunting Traditions
- Sharing
- Compassion
- Humor
- Knowledge of Our Language
- Love and Respect for Elders and One Another
- Spirituality

The natives prominently displayed the values throughout the town. In the hotel, artwork in the elevator centered on the stated values. The values were displayed on the walls above the headboards of beds. Restaurants and schools also listed them. Youth spray-painted the values on dumpsters.

The Iñupiat were a proud people, enriched in ways beyond the material possessions they lacked because of their isolation. Their gratitude was heartwarming; they appreciated our traveling for the field's first game, and they put the best they had to offer on display for us.

There was so much to appreciate about Barrow, despite the challenges the people so evidently faced.

The same radio talk-show host who had conducted a negative interview with me by phone previously also asked to interview me while our group was there. The host had undergone a change of heart toward our project since that initial interview, and before we went on the air, we had a long conversation during which she apologized for being hard on me during out first interview. I was surprised to learn she was from Alabama. She told me how much she loved Barrow, and how living there had made going back to visit her home state during the hot summer months almost unbearable. As we talked, I gained an understanding of why she had pressed me during that first interview. As a host at the only radio station in town, she had her fingers on Barrow's pulse. She knew that as an outsider, I would be met with skepticism. The questions she asked me were the questions her listeners would be asking.

On the way out of the radio station, I noticed a box of partially eaten bags of potato chips. A handwritten sign on the box read, "Take as you need." Our group ate several meals at events related to the game. After meals, uneaten food wasn't taken off the dishes and thrown into the trash. Instead, the leftovers were saved for anyone who would know to come to where we had gathered and eat what remained.

I had never seen anything like that at home or in previous travels. But the acts of looking out for each other, for taking care of those in need, were true to Iñupiat values. My respect for these people and their values increased even more.

CHAPTER 19

FRIDAY NIGHT SUNLIGHT

ame day.

Football, with its one-game-a-week schedule, has a rhythm unique in sports. I'd been through hundreds of football game days as a wife and mom. Each is like a day-long symphony piece, gradually crescendoing from before your feet hit the floor in the morning until the opening kickoff that night.

Except in this case, the buildup began long before alarm clocks went off in Barrow on Friday, August 17. Anticipation for the first Whalers game of the 2007 season had started the previous fall, when their inaugural season ended. Since then, that crescendo had grown exponentially, drawing in new fans and supporters from Jacksonville as well as other parts of the country.

That "Finally!" moment arrived on a chilly, damp, cloudy day in the North Slope.

The media activity began picking up that afternoon with a press conference at the Iñupiat Heritage Center. The national ABC News crew had been joined by TV and newspaper reporters from Anchorage and Fairbanks.

Delbert Rexford, as the foreman, had worked long days making sure the field would be installed in time for the game. Now, wearing a dress shirt and tie for the press conference, he set the tone for the rest of the day when he confidently strolled to the podium and delivered a stirring speech in which he read a letter signed by UIC president Anthony Edwardsen. Delbert had confessed to me that he hadn't always lived a life to be proud of—that was why some of the people in Barrow had wanted him removed from overseeing the field installation. Yet this project proved to be a turning point in Delbert's life.

He read:

Since time immemorial, Iñupiat have adapted to changes within the circumpolar regions of the northern hemisphere in the most severe climatic conditions and elements of nature. We continue to adapt to climatic conditions now and into the future—molding, shaping, and strengthening our unique character as Iñupiat people, developing our mind, and strengthening our body to survive in our environment.

We enter a new era of opportunities for our children as the artificial turf football field is installed and made available for use for our residents, our students, and our children in our community of Barrow. The message we share today is that we are taking a step forward into a new arena to build character and strengthen our Iñupiat values for our children, our youth, and future leaders of tomorrow.

As I listened to Delbert's opening words, I pictured the day only two months earlier when I'd sat in the SchenkelShultz conference room and listened to the UIC board members, one by one, declare, "Now is the time," saving this project from failure.

Delbert continued:

We enter a new era as we have heard the cries of our elders that our children are in dire need of alternative programs and activities to further build their character, dignity, and integrity. Today, this moment, we have in place a football field for our youth and community members as a whole to combat many social ills that attack, destroy, and kill the character of a sound mind and body of a human being.

Ukpeaġvik Iñupiat Corporation embraces the Healthy Communities Initiative on behalf of its shareholders, on behalf of its corporate families, and most importantly the elders who cried for help for our youth, our future, and our community. In the words of Don Shula, "I don't know any other way to lead but by example." UIC leads by example without hesitation to prepare the new field of dreams for our youth, our community, and future leaders of tomorrow.

Today is a historical day for the Iñupiat People. A field of dreams, of hope, of aspirations, of character building and strengthening one's mind and body is now in place. It is an injustice for our Iñupiat to simply sit back when the Healthy Communities Initiative has been declared by our leadership of today to better our Iñupiat society as a whole.

On behalf of the shareholders of UIC, the youth of Barrow, we would like to thank the remarkable Cathy Parker for her vision to make this football field a reality. Cathy, a simple thank you is an injustice for the tremendous efforts you have made to make this day a reality. We thank you with the greatest sincerity and deepest appreciation for what you have done for our community.

Our forefathers and ancestors, the Iñupiat of yesterday, knew a sound mind, a healthy body meant survival in our severe arctic conditions. What you see here today is not just a football field—it is a field of dreams for our youth, our children, and to inspire them to build character. It is a dream that one day will nourish and inspire greatness in our children. In the words of Joe Namath, "Football is an honest game. It's true to life. It's a game about sharing. So is life." Nothing could be truer today because our community shared their resources together to build this football field.

Atauchikun Savakatigiikkapta Pillapiaktugut!!! When we work together we can accomplish anything! On behalf of Ukpeaġvik Iñupiat Corporation and the men and women who worked hard and diligently to make things happen together here in Barrow, I want to take this opportunity to thank each and every person who worked on this field. You built it and I am very proud of your achievement. You were directly involved in a historical project in Barrow's history. Today, this moment, and after the football game, we should not leave this football field without being inspired to work together as a community or the common good of all of our children, all of our youth and community.

Quyanakpak! Thank you very much!

I looked around the room as person after person applauded Delbert's words. I wasn't alone in wiping away tears of joy as I recognized yet another life had been changed through the project.

When it was my turn, I stepped to the podium and received a beautiful blue-and-white parka Susan Hope had made for me. I had trouble keeping my composure to speak through a greater awareness of how much Barrow needed this field.

My desire when I took the microphone was to point out that although thirteen of us had made the trip for the game, there were hundreds of thousands of people who cared about Barrow. I shared several stories of the notes we'd received along with the donations.

"There are people cheering for you," I said, "all over the country."

TRAFFIC JAM IN BARROW

While the press conference was taking place, the final touches were under way on the field, just a couple of hours before the teams would arrive. Turf fields must be swept and dragged to work the rubber mulch down into the surface and to keep the synthetic grass blades upright. Both are essential to ensure proper footing and help prevent injuries. Sweeping and dragging the rubber into the surface is also what gives a field its final, ready-for-action look. That process is accomplished by a rectangular sweeper with broom-like bristles that can be towed around the field by a standard four-wheeler. But the specially designed sweeper didn't arrive in time, forcing the installation crew to improvise by hooking up to the four-wheeler a pair of wood pallets with broom and rake heads screwed to them. I loved their innovation—and it worked!

Although the crews were still working on the field, I was assured that these were finishing touches and that the work would be completed before game time. In fact, because the big work was done, three of the installers from ProGrass asked if their flights could be changed to return home earlier.

"You don't want to stay for the game?" I asked.

"No," one said. "We are ready for fast food and civilization."

I could only imagine how ready they were to go home after living in barracks near the ball field for two weeks and working countless hours under Delbert's leadership.

Once the field had been swept and dragged and the final piece of equipment removed from the playing service, it was finally time for all focus to be on the game.

I didn't learn this until later, but Barrow typically played on Saturday afternoons instead of Friday nights, as we did in the South. It made sense because every game, one of the two teams would have to fly at least five hundred miles to play. But the school scheduled this special game on Friday night for me—to provide a true picture of what I had envisioned from the start of the project. Thanks to extended sunlight that time of year, they could schedule a night game in a stadium without lights.

Most of the town turned out for the game, with estimates as high as three thousand people. Small bleachers were brought in, like what can be seen at youth ball fields, yet many of the spots on the bleachers remained empty because fans preferred to line the field or sit in their cars and trucks around the perimeter.

The orange construction fence was the only barrier surrounding the field, but the Great Wall of China couldn't have held the Barrow fans back that day. There were about twenty feet of turf beyond the sidelines, and many fans chose to stand or place their portable chairs on the turf. One whaling captain actually brought a *lounge chair* and sat it on the edge of the turf. He had the most comfortable seat in the house.

The press box consisted of two plywood pieces painted blue with yellow trim. The bases were the metal cargo boxes carried on semitrailers. The two pieces, with cutout windows, were placed on top of those bases. Two of the media members in the press box came all the way from Pennsylvania for the game and made history of their own. Phil Manney and Tommy Ryan of the Black Diamond Sports Network traveled more than five thousand miles for the first live broadcast of a sports event from above the Arctic Circle. Phil and Tommy were veterans of high school football broadcasts in Pennsylvania, and they said they chose to broadcast the Whalers' game via the internet because they believed in the power of sports and wanted to support the efforts of the people of Barrow.

Alaska's time zone is the Alaska Standard Zone. We had been cautioned that Barrow followed its own unofficial standard of time, with starting times often serving as a mere suggestion. The game was scheduled to begin at 6 p.m., but it didn't start anywhere close to that. That didn't matter, though, because the delayed start gave our

Jacksonville group more time to walk around the stadium and hand out Whalers-blue megaphones with UPS logos that Tom Gloe had brought with him. Plus, I was busy conducting several pregame interviews with reporters who had flown in for the game. The late start also provided extra time for fans caught in a Barrow rarity: a traffic jam, caused by the number of people coming to the game.

Larry Csonka also came, and I was able to talk with him in person for the first time. The members of our group looked awestruck as they asked Larry to autograph their megaphones and a few additional items some had brought from Florida in the hopes of meeting him. Barrow fans were asking me to sign memorabilia too.

"Your fan club line is longer than Larry Csonka's," Brennan Asplen, our principal, teased me.

"Only in Barrow," I responded.

Larry and I walked to midfield together to take part in the pregame coin toss, where we were introduced to the team captains from both teams. The Whalers' opponent, the Seward Seahawks, had flown more than nine hundred miles from south of Anchorage for the game. I received the honor of tossing the coin.

My boys would be so proud of me, I thought as I released the coin into the air. Let me tell you: tossing the coin wasn't as easy as I anticipated. The coin flew about five feet into the air after I released it and landed behind one of the players, who quickly jumped out of the way to avoid the coin's bounce. Neither side asked for a do-over, and the Whalers won the coin toss.

Just before the opening kickoff, I joined members of our Jacksonville group along the sideline to watch the game.

Tom moved around the sideline, blue megaphone in hand, leading the Whalers fans in cheers. Frankly, the fans needed Tom's help. Their lack of football knowledge showed in their uncertainty of exactly when to cheer and when not to. Tom decided to keep matters simple by going with an oldie and a goodie that would work regardless of whether Barrow was on offense or defense: "Two bits, four bits, six bits, a dollar! All for the Whalers, stand up and holler!" The fans, enthused by Tom's interacting with them, stood and hollered on cue.

The Barrow folks didn't need any prompting, however, when their Whalers scored the first points on the new field. In the second quarter, amid a windy mist, Anthony Edwards became the first player to reach the end zone on a short touchdown run that gave Barrow a 6–0 lead. If only the new stadium had had a real scoreboard. Instead, a giant "6" was handwritten on the make-do whiteboard scoreboard—and I mentally added a scoreboard to my list of remaining needs.

Seward, however, was able to erase its deficit by scoring twice in the final four minutes of the first half on a safety and a touchdown run. At halftime, our Whalers trailed 9–6.

HALFTIME SURPRISE

Even my halftime was fully booked. First, I did an interview with Phil and Tom on the internet broadcast. Knowing the game was being aired over the internet to who knows how many different places, I made sure to mention that we still needed to raise money to pay for the field. After all, this was a celebration *and* a business trip.

Before halftime ended, I was asked to stand on the Whalers logo at midfield. Barrow's cheerleaders presented me with a shirt and other gifts. From the press box, one of the Iñupiat elders read a prayer of dedication for the field over the public address system.

The elder opened the prayer by asking God to forgive the community for allowing drugs and alcohol to come into their land and harm their youth. Then he thanked God for providing a beautiful day for the youth to enjoy. He concluded by expressing on behalf of the community its acceptance of the field and its commitment that the field be used to accomplish good.

Tears flowed, yet again. I was wrecked with emotion following the prayer, and then the elder announced to the crowd, "From now on, this field will be called Cathy Parker Field!"

Yep—even more tears!

The people of Barrow had kept their secret well. Previously, I had been in one phone conversation with the UIC's president, when I told him stadiums and fields in the Lower 48 often were named for sponsors and companies. "I think we should name it UIC Field," I casually suggested.

"Maybe one day, when we have an indoor facility," he responded.

Indoor facility? *Uh-oh*, I immediately thought. *I'm not getting involved with that!*

When the elder announced the field's name, I was completely shocked, definitely honored, and a tad bit embarrassed. I didn't deserve that recognition. I had become comfortable as the leader and face of the project, although that required adjustments. But I was part of a team of a few dozen people who were just as committed to bringing the field to Barrow without receiving any credit publicly. Donors from all across the country had made it possible. And, of course, the UIC had saved the project at its most vulnerable moment.

But with my name now on the field, as humbling a moment as that was, I really wanted the Whalers to win this game.

CHAPTER 20

ONE MORE MIRACLE?

There was no way, was there, that the Whalers could lose the first game on their new field? Compared to all the seemingly insurmountable obstacles that had been conquered to get the field in place for the start of the season, their three-point halftime deficit didn't seem like much of a problem to overcome.

Midway through the third quarter, Seward had marched into the Whalers' side of the field when the drive was interrupted by—among the things you would least expect to see during a high school football game next to the Arctic Ocean—a streaker.

A young man, buck naked, sprinted along the sideline on Seward's side of the field.

Vicki Griffis, standing next to me, remarked, "This is a small town. I give it one minute before somebody's going to say who he is."

Sure enough, two seconds later, a Barrow fan near us said, "Oh, that's so-and-so's son."

Before the laughter subsided from the streaker being hauled off by the local authorities, Seward scored on a touchdown pass to take a 16–6 lead with barely more than five minutes left in the third quarter.

As the game moved into the fourth quarter and Barrow still hadn't added any points to that handwritten "6" on their side of the scoreboard, a sinking feeling began to overtake the stadium.

"You know, it's okay if we don't win," Kathy Cope told me. "We are playing a great game."

"Oh, no, this is not okay, Kathy," I said, my competitive spirit coming out in full force. "We need a win!"

The night before the game, our group had eaten dinner with the team's coaches, players, and their families. The players informed me they were dedicating the season to me, starting with the first game. "Well, you'd better win it!" I had jokingly told them. Realistically, I realized they had won only one game the previous year. Thinking they would win their opening game was such a stretch of faith.

None of that reasoning even entered my mind, though, as I stood along the sideline of a field built on steps of faith, one after the other. Having a new field wasn't the only thing that was different about this Whalers team. The players, their coaches, and this community weren't the same. The team had grown not only in knowledge of football through their time at Bartram Trail, but more important, they had witnessed a miracle—and they were standing on it. Many of these players had carried the turf and helped with the installation. I wanted so badly for them to win this game—and knew they wanted to, too—for all the people who had made this day a reality through their donations, work, and prayers.

But time was slipping away. It was time to remember the miracles that had occurred to this point, and to believe for one more. Led by Tom, the crowd started chanting, "Let's go, Whalers!"

Then the Whalers began to mount a late rally. With 2:47 showing on the small digital clock hanging out of the press box window, backup quarterback Albert Gerke, only a sophomore, scored on a 9-yard run. The Whalers, down 16–12, were within a touchdown of winning.

"We're going to have to do an onside kick," Vicki said to me.

I nodded.

"Do you think the other team knows?" Vicki asked.

At that exact moment, the public address announcer declared from the press box, "Now Barrow's going to have to line up and do an onside kick." I'm sure the opposing team's coaches expected Barrow to attempt an onside kick, but still, in all my years of attending football games, I'd never heard a PA announcer say anything like that for an entire stadium to hear.

"Yeah," I said to Vicki. "They know."

Despite the element of surprise being completely removed, the Whalers somehow found a way to recover the onside kick at the Seward 46-yard line. The fans started buzzing at the prospects of a miraculous finish.

The wind had picked up shortly before the opening kickoff, making for a difficult game passing the ball for both teams. But the Whalers' offense, in hurry-up mode as the clock ticked, advanced the ball to the Seahawks' 4-yard line. On the next play, with only thirty-five seconds remaining, Gerke threw a pass toward the end zone. A Seward defender tipped the ball, but it somehow found its way into the hands of Barrow running back Luke George, standing in the center of the end zone.

Touchdown!

I let out my "ugly scream"—head tilted back, eyes closed, gloved hands extended in front of me—loud and with no regard for what my facial expression might be. Pandemonium broke out among the Barrow fans. Car horns blared around the field's perimeter, as fans celebrated from inside their cars. All knew they had just witnessed another against-all-odds miracle.

After the final seconds ticked off the clock, and the Whalers had won 18–16, the fans—almost all of whom had stayed until the end—swarmed the field. The TV cameramen jostled among the rush of fans to get shots of the Barrow players as they celebrated.

Both teams lined up to congratulate each other on a game well played. I overheard a coach from Seward ask, "Can we get a blue field too?"

Some of the Barrow players spotted me, and they hoisted me onto their shoulders as though I were the winning coach. "Miracles, they just keep happening!" I exclaimed over the cheers and celebration. Once the players had lowered me to the ground—gently, thankfully—the players, their fans, and the media members sprinted toward the Arctic Ocean. The players had done the same after their only victory the previous season, but minus all the attention.

I knew better than to follow the crowd, having taken the polar plunge once already. I was a prime candidate to be tossed into the ocean, and I was already cold enough. The cold, wet wind off the water felt like ice hitting my face. Instead, I remained on the field, in the same spot where the players had lowered me from their shoulders, safe and dry, watching as almost everyone else in our group from Jacksonville jumped into the water alongside our Barrow friends. I wanted to stand there and absorb the scene.

Out of the corner of my eye, I noticed a woman walking toward me. I had seen her throughout the game on the opposite side of the field from where I stood, holding a white bedsheet with a note of thanks to me written on it.

"I wanted to make you something, so I took my sheet and I made this for you," she said.

I looked down to the turf. The woman wasn't wearing shoes.

"This is like brand new carpet," she said. "I'm not going to mess it up."

TIME TO REFLECT
AND CELEBRATE

After standing in the wind off the Arctic Ocean for a few hours, I walked into the apartment where Cara and I were staying, instantly appreciating how warm Barrow residents kept their homes. As I thawed out, I started removing the top layers of clothes I'd wrapped myself in for the game. It wasn't long before I needed to open the window to let some of the warm air out! The men from our group called and asked if I wanted to go back to the field. Some of the residents were still there, celebrating, and several from our group wanted to join Trent, Scott Barr, and others in smoking victory cigars.

"Y'all go ahead," I told them. "I'm not going back out."

I stayed in my warm room and reflected on the week, the day, and the game.

During Carl's playing career, I had attended well over a hundred games. I'd been to my sons' youth and high school games. I'd been to championship games that included a Super Bowl and a World Bowl. I'd seen all levels of play in all kinds of circumstances and environments, and I'd become accustomed to hearing fans complain about players' mistakes and second-guess the coaches. But I heard no such complaints during the Whalers' game. Sure, it could have been partly because the fans weren't that well educated on the game of football yet. But I thought to myself—I hoped to myself—that the reason was purer than that: it was simply because the fans wanted to support their team, no matter what, the way it should be. This team, this community, had experienced so much together—good and bad. On this day, the field, the game, the players, and coaches, all had unified a community.

Seward had a good team, and they had what looked like a safe lead against Barrow late in the game. But the Whalers fans' team had won.

And no one could say it was because the Barrow players or coaches had more experience or a history of overcoming adversity to win. I think the fans recognized that their team won because the players owned a ton of heart that merged with a sudden boost of momentum to form an unbeatable force. The Whalers players and coaches had won because of what they possessed inside of them. They had earned the victory not because of what they had done, but because of who they were.

Then I thought about the fans back in Jacksonville who, from a time zone four hours ahead, had been keeping up with the game. It was too late there to call back home. I assumed that many had gone to bed when the outcome looked bleak. I could picture their reactions in the morning when they woke up and heard the final score: "Oh my gosh! We won!"

I typed out emails on the computer in the apartment. I had just witnessed another miracle, and I had to tell my family and friends back home, even if they wouldn't learn about until a few hours later. I was thankful that media had captured on film and in photos what we had witnessed. I was thankful that the guys from Black Diamond Sports had traveled from Pennsylvania to broadcast the game. But still, I felt a personal responsibility to share the outcome with all who had contributed to this victory.

I drifted off to sleep, continuing to reflect on the day, praying that the Barrow Whalers would see many more days like this one.

REVELING IN THE VICTORY

The next morning, we stopped by the store that not only was where residents could purchase everything from groceries to four-wheelers to clothing, but also served as the local hangout. There had been people so excited about the win that they had stayed out all night.

Four Barrow players were sitting on the store's front steps, still wearing their white jerseys from the night before. The store faced the main road through town, making it the perfect location for a group of players to achieve their goal of being recognized as the players from the winning football team.

It was a great day to be a Barrow Whaler.

I stopped in the parking lot to savor the moment too—watching the players, who still had far more energy than even I had after my full night's rest. I'd be leaving for home the next day, along with the rest of our group from Jacksonville. We still had more money to raise, but our work in Barrow was done. The field was in place. It was Barrow's now.

I knew in my heart and mind both: Barrow football was not just going to survive another season. It was going to thrive and breathe new life into this community for years to come.

CHAPTER 21

CLOSING THE BOOKS

With the field in place and properly christened, all that remained for Project Alaska was to complete the funding.

Larry Csonka and I had been asked to speak in Anchorage at a fund-raiser, which had been set up by the businessman who had showed up in Barrow with the $40,000 check to finish paying for the team's trip to Jacksonville. While the rest of our group returned home, Kathy and I stopped over in Anchorage on Sunday to attend the fund-raiser.

The *Anchorage Daily News* in the Anchorage airport had an account of the game on its front page. I read the paper's coverage with interest, because that paper had previously not been favorable toward our efforts when I'm sure they thought our crazy idea would never become reality. The coverage of the game was all positive and portrayed the Whalers team, the people in Barrow, and even me in a good light.

Before the fund-raiser, I took part in a few radio show interviews, all the while plugging our website so people could learn how to donate.

Before the event, Larry and Audrey met Kathy and me at a restaurant. Larry, sitting across from me, engaged me in conversation, leaving Audrey and Kathy to talk among themselves.

Larry asked me point-blank, "Why did you want to make this field happen?"

Larry is a physically massive man, and as his eyes bored into mine, I felt that the question represented a credibility test to determine whether my motives were pure and my intentions all along had been to honor the people of Barrow.

I gave Larry a lengthy answer, explaining to him about our family's involvement in sports, Carl's coaching, and the comments we heard from our players' families, thanking us for investing in the lives of their sons. I recounted the Sunday morning we had watched the ESPN story, and how I hadn't been able to get what I had seen from Barrow out of mind. As I described the passion for a team and a town I'd never heard of, Larry leaned back comfortably in his seat, continuing to listen. I had passed his test.

Larry and I also talked about the group of opponents who had become a thorn in my side. I told him how they had blocked us from putting the field where we intended, and how some of their emails hurt me. As Larry quietly listened, I admitted I was still upset by the opponents.

"I know it is very frustrating to you," Larry said. "But those people live there. That is their land, their community. You don't have to live there. You don't understand what they have to deal with. You could be more negative, or you could gain their understanding."

Larry was correct, and I translated his words as, *You need to be gracious and keep your mouth shut.* I trusted Larry because of how connected he'd become to Barrow. He understood the people there as well as any outsider could. I had no intention of being negative with the media about our opponents. That's not my nature. But I needed to stop letting the opposition bother me. Where I lacked understanding, I needed to display grace and compassion by choosing to honor the people who opposed us. Who knew? I might never step foot in Barrow again. But they lived and worked there. It was their home. And Barrow needed its residents to rally together around their youth, not be divided over a football field.

TOUGH ACT TO FOLLOW

The fund-raiser took place at the Petroleum Club, an elegant business club in the heart of Anchorage that was almost intimidating when I first walked in. *Petroleum Club?* I thought. *How much money do you need to have to be a member of the* Petroleum *Club?* The invitation list consisted of a who's who of Anchorage business leaders. I'd been told the event would have appetizers, not a meal. When I saw the buffet of heavy appetizers that included one of my favorite food groups, seafood, I knew somebody was shelling out some money for this event. I didn't eat, because I was nervous and knew I needed to be ready to shake hands and meet people.

Larry spoke first and did an amazing job of describing Friday night's game and the residents of Barrow's enthusiasm for the field. He recounted how the Whalers had won, telling the crowd that right after the winning touchdown, a little boy next to him looked up and boasted, "That's my cousin!"

Because of all that Larry had done for the state and his inclusion in the Pro Football Hall of Fame, he could have shown up to that fund-raiser and said, "Hi, everybody," and he would have had everyone's undivided attention. But through the heartfelt manner with which he talked about the game and his relationship with Barrow's football program, Larry had the crowd eating out of his hands.

I listened intently to Larry's words, captivated by every word he shared about his experiences with the Barrow Whalers, but simultaneously wondering how in the world I was going to follow him to the microphone.

Then Larry shifted gears. Still speaking from the heart, but with a hint of bewilderment in his voice, he said, "You all need to be ashamed. This lady has raised this money and is doing this from Florida, and you all need to step up and help her."

Oh my gosh! I can't believe he actually said that! I thought. Yet, there was truth to his words. We had secured buy-in from around the country, but we needed these people's support to complete the fund-raising. I just was not accustomed to such bold honesty when it came to asking people for money. Thank God that Larry was fearless enough to ask for it. I prayed Larry's words would stir their hearts toward this end rather than offend.

I swallowed hard as I stood up to approach the stage, now even more anxious to follow Larry. I looked over the audience of about seventy-five to gauge their reactions to Larry's challenge, and gratefully was met with a roomful of kind faces. When I reached the microphone, I started with my story of how I'd learned about Barrow's need for a football field. I talked about watching ESPN before church, and how with each person I spoke with, it became clearer that I needed to listen to the voice calling me toward action, toward helping the people of Barrow. I could sense the audience moved with emotion as I described how our community had wanted to help even though we were four thousand miles away, and then how other parts of Florida and then the Lower 48 had become involved. I shared some of the comments and letters we had received, and how people who donated said they were thrilled by the opportunity to make a difference even though it would be in a place where their kids would not benefit, or they, themselves, would never see in person.

I noticed people wiping their eyes as I talked about how we shared a desire to provide the best for our youth, regardless of where we lived. I'm sure they were each reflecting on their own stories. Perhaps they'd had an opportunity to play sports and learned much from it. Perhaps they had not had an opportunity to participate in sports and, from that perspective, understood the importance of providing a chance for someone else. Their stories would vary, but I had seen many times from audiences in Florida the same look of wanting to be a part of something that would make a difference in others' lives.

Larry gave a tug on their wallets, and I gave a tug on their hearts.

Afterward, I don't think anyone left the room without asking Kathy or me how they could invest in the project. Numerous people thanked me for what I had done. Several told me they would support the project. When we had talked with the last person from the crowd, I was completely confident we'd bring in the rest of more than $100,000 we needed.

We closed the books on the project about a month after returning home—and before the Whalers' season had ended. We continued working on a scoreboard for the field. With a donation from Wells Fargo and transportation from UPS, a new scoreboard and twenty-five-second play clock were installed in time for the Whalers' next season.

None of us who worked so diligently on raising the funds or the field took it for granted when we were able to say, "It is finished." We had experienced yet another miracle along the journey of completing this story.

CHAPTER 22

NO DESIRE FOR NORMAL

The wave of media attention following the game splashed all the way from Barrow to Jacksonville.

ESPN produced an *Outside the Lines* segment featuring Barrow's new field, and that episode aired several times around the Thanksgiving holiday. Even after we paid off the field, I received more speaking and interview requests, and I obliged as much as my schedule allowed because I never grew tired of telling the story and observing how it encouraged people.

In the days after the field had been paid off, I finally had time to slow down and reflect on all that had happened. I had many people to thank for their support and help. I owed a debt of gratitude to the transportation companies involved, especially after seeing firsthand Barrow's inaccessibility, and realized the significance of the challenge they were asked to perform.

Brad, Ike, Tom, and Kathy often joined me at speaking engagements and enthusiastically told their side of the fascinating story. The more we told the story, the more we comprehended how miraculous it was. Reactions from audiences seeing for the first time a photo of the completed field sitting next to the Arctic Ocean confirmed we had been a part of something out of the ordinary. I grasped for the first time the compressed timeline with which we had worked. In a span of only six months, the project-launching press conference led to completion of a football field with an estimated value of goods and services far greater than the $500,000 we had originally estimated—signed, sealed, and delivered for the community of Barrow to enjoy.

A defining moment for me came when I told the story at one event, and the CEO of a logistics company approached me afterward and said, "I want to tell you that if I put all my staff and all our resources on that one project, we couldn't have done that. It's impossible to pull off that type of project in that amount of time."

"I know," I told the CEO. "It was only through God."

The story lifted my own faith each time I shared it. On one occasion, I was tired from a long day at the office when I arrived at an evening speaking engagement. After speaking, I left the event energized. Proverbs 11:25 came alive to me: "A generous person will prosper; whoever refreshes others will be refreshed."

A friend who pastored a church near Athens, Georgia, asked me to speak as part of the church's launch of an emphasis on missions. I spoke after the service at a covered-dish lunch in the fellowship hall. Afterward, an elderly man came to me, tears in his eyes.

"Cathy, years ago, I felt like God told me to do something," he said. "Because nobody else thought it was a good idea, I didn't do it. You have so inspired me to do it anyway."

We built that field for Barrow. But God also used the story of the field to reach people in places far from Barrow, like that sweet little man, late in his life, who wasn't going to leave earth feeling defeated because he heard the story and decided to do what God had called him to do.

I would hear so many more testimonies like the elderly man's that had nothing to do with football. One that impacted me the most came from a young mother who had heard me early in the process speak of my desire to help Barrow. She stopped me at a ball field about a year after the project had concluded.

"We don't know each other very well," she said, "but I want to tell you how your story impacted me." She described how her eight-year-old son had struggled with complications from cancer and had been hospitalized for an extended time with little hope of recovering. At her son's lowest point, she had cried out to God to increase her faith that miracles can happen.

"That is when I saw your story of the field's completion on the news. Your story gave me the faith to believe another night."

Taken aback, all I could ask was, "How is your son doing?"

She pointed to a boy running around. "That's him."

Wow! To think, there were many points in the journey when this determined Southern gal had been mad at God for giving me the idea and thinking that it had ruined me. Ultimately, though, I am so grateful that God chose me and that He gave me the ability and determination to see Project Alaska through to the end.

THE AFTERMATH

As time passed following that first game on the field in Barrow, I realized all the more what a miracle that field really was. Then, as I began to hear of the success stories coming out of Barrow—how lives were changing there, and even how lives outside of Barrow and Jacksonville both were being impacted by this story—all the work and stress and hassles seemed worthwhile.

I closely followed Barrow's season, including the updates our local papers printed because of the ongoing interest. The Whalers lost their second and third games of the season, but they won three of their final four games to finish the season with a 4–3 record.

I maintained regular contact with Trent, Susan, Coach Voss, and Coach Houston back in Barrow. Players from both teams stayed in touch through emails, phone calls, and social media.

I heard accounts of how perceptions of Barrow changed because of the positive publicity that came from the first game on the field. Communities in the North Slope in general weren't looked at favorably. The villages, as they were often called, were perceived around Alaska as having too much handed to them. "They don't deserve it" was a common complaint.

Yet now, I was hearing from people who said they flew to Barrow for the sole purpose of watching a football game there. One man emailed to say his grandfather was eighty and confined to a wheelchair. The grandfather told his family, "Before I leave this earth, I want to go and see a ball game on the Barrow field." His grandson wrote to me, "I just wanted you to know that we're taking Grandpa to Barrow."

An educator in Barrow sent an email that wound up circulating through our local school system and the board of education. She told me, "We miss you already, but you left us a symbol of hope and faith." She said on days when she became discouraged, she would walk the field to find encouragement. "Today," she wrote, "I stood alone on the field of dreams, closed my eyes, and felt the power of God."

Being a player on the Barrow football team became a source of pride. While flying to away games, the Whalers were often stopped in airports when passersby recognized them as "that team with the new blue field."

Residents proudly claimed they were from Barrow. They had a renewed pride in their heritage and wanted to display it more often. Susan Hope told me that at games, Iñupiat dancers began performing native dances, accompanied by drummers, as a way to honor old traditions among the new. Even Susan's nephew—the one who had expressed disdain for touching whale because non-natives would mock him at school for smelling like it—was feeling renewed pride in Iñupiat customs as people from outside the community grew increasingly fascinated by them. The attention from outsiders who wanted to understand Barrow's culture ignited a belief among the youth that their culture was cool. Football helped bridge the gap between natives and non-natives.

Football did not change Barrow. Sowing into its youth changed Barrow. Football provided the avenue. It brought them hope.

The impact was felt in the Jacksonville community too. Bartram Trail High School was seven years old, and the media attention brought name recognition to our school. Bartram embraced its identity as the school that helped the Barrow team, and the project highlighted the values of service that Coach Sutherland had been working hard to instill in our team. Still, it wasn't just the students who learned a lesson about service. The parents, too, learned a rest-of-their-life lesson about the impact that comes from serving others.

While our Jacksonville group was in Barrow for the field's opening, we were presented a twelve-foot long piece of baleen—like a set of bristles in a whale's mouth that works as a filter-feeder system. The baleen represented how whaling crews went out into the ocean and worked together, risking their lives to sustain the community. It was given to us so that we would remember the Barrow football team. When we returned home, Tom Gloe presented the baleen to the Bartram Trail football team and explained its significance. An arch was built behind one of our field's end zones, and the baleen was suspended from that arch so each of our players could reach up and touch it each time they entered the field and remember the concept of teamwork it stood for.

The Bartram football team went 9–5 that season, losing in overtime in the state semifinals. Seven players from that team signed NCAA Division I football scholarships. Xavier Brewer went to

Clemson with Kyle, where they remained teammates. Kyle Griffis received an appointment to West Point. For his nomination interview during the admissions process, his topic was a life-changing experience. He chose to talk about his involvement in the Barrow project.

NEW PLACES TO IMPACT

I'm a "What's next?" type of person. In the aftermath of the project accomplishing its goal, I had to accept that Barrow no longer needed me to have a successful football program. That with the field in place, the people of Barrow were okay on their own. As a mother, that was difficult, because we mommas always want to feel needed.

In a conversation with Vicki, I said, "I don't think I can go back to just life as usual." The project had represented enormous steps of faith and stretched my belief that God does big, huge things through people who obey His calling. The project made a tremendous impact, and not only in Barrow.

"I just don't want to go back to a normal life," I told her.

On the flights to Barrow, when there was ample time to think, I had sensed God giving me what would become the mission statement for a new nonprofit: "EQUIP communities with the resources necessary to assist athletic programs, INSPIRE coaches and leaders to become mentors of young athletes, and DEVELOP character in young athletes, encouraging them to share their God-given talents."

I looked around at the group with me on the plane. One of the best architects in his industry and one of the best transportation specialists in his business had partnered with me. An attorney well versed in nonprofit tax laws had attended one of my speaking engagements and offered his services free of charge. I had worked alongside the best of the best. And then, of course, I had been surrounded by faithful prayer warriors and difference makers in my community.

There's a lot more we can do, I concluded.

Back home after the trip, I attended a meeting for an education foundation board on which I served. A friend and respected school board member approached me, kindly saying, "If you never do another thing, when you stand before God, He's going to say, 'Well done, good and faithful servant.'"

I smiled and thanked her, yet after the meeting, when I returned to my car and replayed the conversation in my mind before driving home, I found myself in tears. "God," I cried, "please don't let this be the last thing I do for You."

With further reflection I began to realize that when you come off a major project, like I had with Project Alaska, you can't help but question whether you'll ever be part of anything big again. I couldn't imagine being involved in another project that would receive as much attention as Project Alaska, and I had to accept that to keep moving forward. But I also believed I could take on other ventures. That I and the others I'd grown close to through our work together weren't finished yet.

All of this self-reflection led to the creation in 2008 of Athletes to Champions, a grassroots nonprofit created with some of the same team from the field project to help kids build character, learn discipline, and value respect through sports. Many of the parents who'd helped with the field project volunteered to work with our new nonprofit.

One of our first projects was sending a group of Bartram Trail players and coaches to Barrow that summer to conduct a football camp. I had promised Dave and Collin that Collin could go if they made Bs and Cs in school. As the group to fly to Barrow was formed, it became apparent several of our host families had made similar promises. Flights were almost $2,000 per person because of high fuel costs at the time. We had buy-in from our school, but we were going to have to come up with $22,000 for the trip. I felt sure we could accomplish this through Athletes to Champions, even though we were a start-up with no money in the bank.

One player's mom got upset with me, telling me, "You have got to quit making promises. We need to have money in the bank before you make any promises."

The mom was correct; we did need to have the money in the bank before I made any promises. But once again, I had found myself with a vision much bigger than logic. Oh, how I wished we could have money in the bank! And how I wished God preferred to tell me what He wanted me to do with money I'd already raised instead of telling me what He wanted me to do before I raised the money.

But where is the faith in that?

PROMISE FULFILLED

Soon afterward, I received a request to speak at a small town in Georgia where a church was hosting a luncheon for the community. I told the story of the field, yet didn't ask for one penny. As I spoke, I noticed an elderly man in the audience crying. Afterward, a lady from the town approached me, telling me the man had asked if my nonprofit could accept stock as a donation. When the stock was cashed out a few weeks later, it came to a little over $22,000—exactly what we needed to send ten of our coaches and players to Barrow for the camp.

It was only fitting that Coach Sutherland lead that trip. He worked with Brian Houston, the Barrow coach, to perfect the skills they had worked on the previous summer. Collin was privileged to be part of the group. I was nervous that once Collin experienced the hunting and fishing available in Barrow, he might not return. Especially since he was visiting during the warmer months. The entire group did return with photos and stories they could cherish for a lifetime. By the way, both Bartram Trail and Barrow reached their state semifinals that season.

A2C, as we called the nonprofit for short, initially focused its attention on athletic programs in Jacksonville and the surrounding area by putting on sports camps. We helped start-up teams pay league fees and purchase uniforms and equipment. We set up concession stands where teams could raise money. Kyle enjoyed seeing the impact we were making, and after he became better known regionally as starting quarterback in football and key player on the baseball team at Clemson, we tapped into his connections to hold camps in South Carolina and North Carolina. Athletes he became friends with helped coach at the clinics.

I was surprised one day when approached by the leader of a new ministry out of North Carolina called Power Cross. The founders, Jeff and Natalie Storment, had watched the ESPN special on the completed Barrow field and reached out to me hoping we could share ideas and resources. That led to an amazing partnership. Carl, Kyle, and several former Bartram players provided football and baseball camps for Power Cross youth. Kyle would later host a group from Power Cross at Clemson and treat them to Tigers baseball and football games. Cara and Kendal also pitched in as camp counselors at each A2C Sports Character Camp.

For almost a decade, A2C, with heavy support from Winn-Dixie and other partners, accomplished much through its projects. In 2018, we changed our nonprofit's name to Beyond the Ballfield, with the same purpose of empowering athletes to use their influence for good.

What began as one field for one team in one town birthed a new way of impacting individuals and communities through sports. I'm grateful that the restlessness inside of me wouldn't allow me to settle for a "normal" life again, and that I was able to see that sports could bring unity. I wouldn't say that God has called me to "bigger and better" things since the Barrow project, because I'm not sure I would want to know what would be bigger than putting a football field above the Arctic Circle. But God definitely has called me to do more, like being a coach's wife and all that offers through being around youth and sports.

I always want to be obedient to His calling, discovering each next step for following Him as I go.

CHAPTER 23

A NEW BARROW

Carl and I took the final step off the stairs and onto the tarmac at the Barrow airport. This was an all-new experience for Carl as he made his first trip to northern Alaska. In some ways, this trip eleven years after that inaugural game on the blue field was a new experience for me too. The Barrow of 2018 wasn't the same Barrow I'd first visited in 2007, and I couldn't wait to see the difference and show off the town to my husband.

Our reason for this first trip together came as the result of the miracle God had worked in our marriage. We had been married more than thirty years and had seen more than our share of ups and downs. We had faced obstacles that can destroy a marriage. Now, one of Barrow's churches had invited Carl and me to speak in a Sunday service and then—of all things—a marriage workshop. When I told a friend my surprise at our being asked to help other people improve their marriages, he told me, "Well, there's nothing y'all haven't been through."

I'd been to Barrow two other times since the field opened. Of course, I'd stayed in contact with a number of people through the years. Trent Blankenship had returned to work in the Lower 48 in 2009. Coach Voss had retired, and Brian Houston had also served a stint as head coach. Carl and I had been thrilled to see Brian receive that opportunity.

In one of my visits, I'd met the new superintendent of the school district. He informed me that the dropout rate for students who entered the high school in ninth grade—that key statistic when the football program was started—had dropped to 0 percent. He added that daily attendance and the student involvement level had continued to increase.

To coincide with one of my visits, the 2007 team gathered for a pizza party/team reunion, with many of the players attending. Several from that team had gone off to college or moved away from Barrow, but most of those had come back because they loved Barrow and wanted to raise families there.

It was so rewarding to see what remarkable young men they had become, and how they were productive citizens in their community.

Dave Evikana was at the reunion. He had encountered a rough spot for a few years and had been incarcerated, but he was back on the right track by then and proudly boasted about his son to me.

I met two alumni who weren't part of that '07 team. They were Samoans who had moved to Barrow in, best as I recall, 2010. They were huge guys, and they were wonderful young men. Their father had moved the family there from Hawaii. Imagine that culture shock!

The father had been trying to convince his boys that he wasn't ruining their lives by moving them to Barrow, but they weren't buying. A football coach met the father and sons at the airport. The coach had to be thanking God for sending two big boys like them to Barrow. The first item on the agenda was to take the boys to see the field. Not the school, not where they were going to live—the field!

When I met the boys, they both hugged me and thanked me.

One told me, "We had a great high school experience, and we wouldn't have if we didn't have football."

I also had attended one big Whalers football game without traveling to Barrow.

In 2017, the Whalers advanced to the state championship game near Anchorage. They'd also qualified for the championship game in 2011, but had lost to finish as runners-up. This time, they won their first state championship, stopping their opponent at the 2-yard line on the final play of the game to win 20–14. I couldn't have imagined witnessing anything cooler than the program that at one time had been on the verge of being canceled winning a state title.

But then it got better. After the game, the Whalers were announced as recipients of the award for having the highest team grade-point average in the state.

The Barrow football program helps develop smart, young men who represent their school and community well.

BACK TO THE FIELD

Football seasons had prevented Carl from joining me on my previous trips. Ironically, football season actually enabled Carl to join me this time. He was back to coaching high school football, in Georgia, and a statewide mandatory "dead week" for football activities in July provided a break on his calendar to come with me.

Just as in 2007, the first stop after leaving the airport had to be the field.

I took quick note that the blue and yellow still popped from among the shades of gray, but this time, I was more interested in Carl's reactions.

"This is beautiful!" he said.

Carl walked halfway across the field before getting down on his knees and touching the turf. "It's in great shape," he said.

He swiped his hands across the field.

"The fibers feel like they were just installed."

A field like this one typically has a life span of ten to twelve years. The fields back home for which Carl had overseen the installation were in the process of being replaced. The two major causes of field deterioration are heat and sunlight. Guess what? Barrow doesn't get much heat and sunlight.

As Carl and I walked across the field together, we noticed ripples that were signs of divots below the surface. The shifting ground caused by the thawing of the permafrost might require lifting the turf to level underneath it. There also might be a need to add rubber mulch soon. But the turf itself didn't appear as though it will need to be replaced anytime in the near future.

The football program was in good shape too. I was able to introduce Carl to the current head coach, Chris Battle, who had led the Whalers to the state championship the year before. Carl and Chris hit it off and enjoyed talking football together.

Carl went back during our stay to watch the football players' off-season workouts. It was during the Fourth of July holiday. I don't know if all the players were working out, but a bunch were.

"I'm impressed," Carl said. "They're showing up and working out."

OBSERVING THE DIFFERENCES

During our trips around town, I would point out to Carl how Barrow had changed over eleven years. Brian Houston served as our host and showed us a new hospital with very nice-looking facilities. And a new hotel. The number of buildings appeared to have doubled.

The town was cleaner too.

"There was a lot of trash on the ground my first time here," I told Carl. "Now I don't see any trash anywhere. They've really cleaned up the town."

I enjoyed catching up with old friends and finally being able to introduce them to Carl. Of course, we had opportunities to talk with plenty of people at the church.

Our trip coincided with Barrow's annual Independence Day festivities, which have a fair-like atmosphere while the sun is out almost all day. The Eskimo Games are part of the festivities. The Games include foot races and games of strength, but there also are amusing games, like the two-foot high kick, which consists of jumping and touching a suspended target with both feet and then landing on both feet without falling to the ground. Carl and I were astonished by the ear pull. Two competitors sat facing each other. Each had a string looped around one of his ears, and they pulled on the string using their ears until either the string came off one of their ears or one conceded because of the pain. (We chose not to sample the ear pull.) Winners at the Eskimo Games can advance to the World Eskimo Indian Olympics.

The public address announcer informed the people that Carl and I were there. I lost track of how many people took pictures with us. They treated us like we were famous!

Of all the differences I noticed in Barrow, the most fulfilling were in the people themselves. They still battle issues, as every community does. Alcoholism remains a problem, but there's a rehab facility there now. Jobs are plentiful and pay well, making the North Slope an enticing area to move to. Along with the changes, the need to be a subsistence society is decreasing. However, the natives' love for whaling remains. The Iñupiat culture is important to them, and they will have to intentionally keep their culture a driving force in who they are collectively as a people. It will be important for them to maintain their heritage and educate their youth, especially in the Iñupiat values.

In faces all across town, in faces of all ages, I saw a look of hope for a bright future. Now Barrow brims with an immeasurable sense of hope. There's a pride that's come with the knowledge that people all across the country care about them.

I'm not assigning all credit to the football field. I've worked with youth organizations for over a decade, and I have observed that when a community pours into its youth, the future improves, often rapidly.

A community that leads its youth will eventually follow its youth.

I've talked with a coach whose team has competed against Barrow. He told me, "I want you to know what an impact that field had. We had already talked among other teams that were scheduled to play Barrow after that first season that they played on gravel. We'd already said, 'We will never go there and play them. If they want to play, they're going to have to come to us.' The field was too risky to have our kids play on that surface. We weren't going to subject our kids to that. Secondly, it was not a place that we liked going. The reputation there was not good."

When the shift in Barrow came, the coach added, it was profound and noticed by everyone.

"Now, if we have to play an away game there," he said, "it's one of our favorite destination games."

Other communities in Alaska have started football programs of their own, even putting in artificial turf fields for their teams. The reason consistently cited: they saw the changes in Barrow and wanted what Barrow had become.

REASON TO BELIEVE

When I review my original plan to have a few large sports companies write big checks to pay for the Barrow field, I realize how short-sighted my initial vision was. Looking back over the records of all the donations for the Barrow field, it's amazing to see the buy-in that came from so many different people, from so many different walks of life.

I think back to a coworker at the bank. He had just come on board to help start the bank, and I barely knew him. He wasn't even drawing a salary yet. Yet he came into my office and handed me an envelope. "I've got something for your project that you're doing," he said. I opened the envelope to see a personal check for $2,000.

Toward the end of the project, a local couple mailed a check along with a letter in which the husband explained that when they heard about our project, the wife remarked that she believed their sons' involvement in sports was the reason they never found themselves in serious trouble growing up. The husband told his wife that for his Christmas present to her, he would donate $500 in her name. The wife told him to make the check out for $1,000, and that they would place a picture of the field under their Christmas tree.

One of my favorite conversations was with Nancy Parrot, who has since passed away. "Ms. Nancy" was a sweet widow of a doctor from southern Georgia and a perfect Southern belle. She donated to the project and was one of our faithful prayer warriors. One day, Ms. Nancy asked me, "How are our boys in Barrow doing?" The way she said "our boys," made me smile. Those boys were hers as much as they were mine. She had prayed for the project and donated money to help them. Everything I was doing for the project was as much about her as it was me. And there were people this could be said of all over the country. We all shared a bond through Barrow.

God's plan was better. The impact was much greater than two communities. I'll never meet all the people who were a part of the project. I'll never even know who they are. But God does.

THE HAND OF THE LORD

If I am proof of anything, it's that God works through those who are willing to heed His call. I can't imagine a more unlikely person to lead the Barrow field project than a busy wife and mom with four children and a full-time job. Until Project Alaska, I had never raised money and never been the person onstage, motivating people to support a cause. I wasn't very business savvy. I wasn't wealthy, super connected, or exceptionally smart. I wasn't an obvious choice—at least by my standards—for doing this work.

That there is a blue-and-yellow football field in Barrow, Alaska, points not to my abilities, but to God's.

I made plenty of mistakes during the project. I am so ordinary. That's why writing this book was important to me. That's why I wanted to not only tell the complete story of how that cool-looking field wound up in Barrow, but also show my flaws and the mistakes I've made. I mean this with all sincerity and humility: if God can write an amazing story through me, He can do the same through you.

He wants to.

If you feel as if God has told you to do something and you can't shake it, if it's the first thing that comes to your mind in the morning and the last thing on your mind when you go to bed, it's probably because you are the person He has called to do it.

It's you.

Don't try to give it away to someone else. Don't think it's impossible.

Perhaps the reason God has tapped you on the shoulder is because He wants you to do something you've never done before, that you're not capable of doing without Him, that will stretch you further than you've ever been stretched. You also will grow closer to Him than you've ever been.

And you'll be amazed by what God will do.

APPENDIX 1

2007 BARROW WHALERS ROSTER

No.	Player	Position
2	Cody Romine	Quarterback/Strong Safety
4	Taylor Elbert	Fullback/Linebacker
6	Mikey Stotts	Receiver/Cornerback
8	Anthony Edwards	Running Back/Linebacker
9	Albert Gerke	Receiver/Free Safety
12	Justin Sanders	Receiver/Free Safety
13	Daniel Thomas	Quarterback/Free Safety
15	Adrian Panigeo	Receiver/Cornerback
18	Van Derrick Edwardsen	Receiver/Cornerback
20	Jim Martin	Receiver/Cornerback
21	Dave Evikana	Receiver/Cornerback
22	Austin Fishel	Receiver/Cornerback
26	Cody Gleason	Tight End/Defensive End
28	Jarid Hope	Fullback/Linebacker
30	Nathanial Snow	Receiver/Cornerback
31	Luke George	Running Back/Linebacker
32	Ganinna Pili	Receiver/Cornerback
34	Mac Rock	Receiver/Strong Safety
38	Robert Vigo	Right Back/Strong Safety
54	Joe Burke	Offensive Line/Defensive Line
56	Zac Rohan	Offensive Line/Defensive Line
57	Tim Barr	Offensive Line/Defensive Line
59	Robin Kaleak	Offensive Line/Defensive Line
62	Jason Ruckle	Tight End/Defensive End
66	Alastair Dunbar	Offensive Line/Defensive Line
68	John Wilson	Offensive Line/Defensive Line
69	Forrest Ahkiviana	Offensive Line/Defensive End
72	Kiefer Kanayurak	Offensive Line/Defensive Line
73	Mike Gonzales	Offensive Line/Defensive Line
74	Trevor Litera	Offensive Line/Defensive Line
75	Mike Olson	Offensive Line/Defensive Line
76	John Lambrecht	Offensive Line/Defensive Line
77	Dane Enoch	Offensive Line/Defensive End

78	Colton Blankenship	Offensive Line/Defensive Line
79	Denver Enoch	Offensive Line/Defensive Line
80	Forest Enlow	Receiver/Cornerback

Head Coach: Mark Voss

Assistant Coaches: Jeremy Arnhart, Brian Houston, Brad Igou

2007 BARTRAM TRAIL BEARS VARSITY ROSTER

No.	Player	Position
2	Nick Smith	Wide Receiver
3	Kalup Fewox	Running Back
4	Austin Luongo	Outside Linebacker
5	Mark Safer	Defensive Back
6	Derrick Taylor	Running Back
7	Blake Thomas	Defensive Back
8	Kyle Parker	Quarterback
9	Xavier Brewer	Defensive Back
10	Alex Douglas	Linebacker
11	Darius Lawrence	Linebacker
12	Jason Young	Quarterback
15	Andrew Parker	Tight End
17	Josh Arnwine	Tight End
18	Kyle Griffis	Quarterback
20	Ryan Sidawi	Running Back
21	Will Goebel	Kicker
22	Terrell Ford	Running Back
23	Taylor Johnson	Running Back
27	Damon Lawrence	Defensive Back
28	Matt Youngs	Running Back
30	Josh Malandrucco	Defensive Back
31	Nick Jones	Linebacker
33	Trey Chesser	Defensive Back
34	Colin McQuillen	Outside Linebacker
40	Zach Romani	Linebacker
41	Kevin Kroper	Defensive Back
42	Anthony Luongo	Linebacker
44	Trey Sumner	Outside Linebacker
45	Tyler Smith	Linebacker
45	Evan Hall	Running Back
46	Marshall McMillan	Outside Linebacker
47	Tanner Creed	Defensive Line
50	Adam Butler	Linebacker
51	Dustin Bishop	Linebacker
52	Fransisco Sierra	Defensive Line

53	Aaron Peterman	Offensive Line
54	Christian DeTrude	Defensive Line
55	John Watts	Offensive Line
56	Greg Robertson	Offensive Line
57	Brad Frost	Linebacker
58	Jonathan Linkenheimer	Kicker
59	Matt Williams	Defensive Line
60	Kevin Itner	Offensive Line
61	Cody Shostrom	Offensive Line
62	Kevin Wakley	Defensive Line
63	Brad Waldron	Offensive Line
64	David Triassi	Offensive Line
65	Jarred Kanta	Offensive Line
66	William Ten Eyck	Offensive Line
67	Robert Shannon	Defensive Back
70	Drew Doxzon	Offensive Line
75	Matthew Bernstein	Offensive Line
79	Grant Horner	Offensive Line
80	Matt Markowitz	Wide Receiver
81	Collin Parker	Wide Receiver
82	Brad Poor	Wide Receiver
85	Charles Bailey	Wide Receiver
88	Nathan Pierschke	Wide Receiver
89	Xavier Zayas	Wide Receiver
99	Tyler Tayse	Defensive Line

Head Coach: Darrell Sutherland

Offensive Coordinator: Carl Parker

Defensive Coordinator: Ed Snyder

Assistant Coaches: Trevor Abbs, Brian Ferguson, Travis Hodge, Rob Jennis, Marc Nadeau, Mike Poyer, Lou Seward, Carl Smith, Mel Stowers, Ben Windle

ACKNOWLEDGMENTS

Thank you to:

My husband: You say to me every day the words, "I love you." But so much more important, you show me. I'm so thankful to be on this journey with you, and I'm also thankful to know that God is still working in and through us. Thank you for encouraging me to share the good and the bad in hopes of helping others. You are making a huge impact in this world every day as a coach, husband, and father, and I am so thankful to be by your side.

My mom and dad: Thank you for showing me how to serve. You both have been great examples of how to give with a cheerful heart.

My children: Thank you for allowing me to share our lives with others, especially the lessons learned at the ballfields. I love you dearly.

My brothers and sisters: We are so blessed to have each other. Thank you for pushing me to never give up.

My business partners: Honnie and Darren, thank you for opening the doors to tell this story.

My friends: Thank you for loving me and my family. Especially to Cassie, Margi, and Paula: Thank you for investing your time and resources into helping me tell this story.

My Alaskan friends: Thank you for sharing your lives with a complete stranger four thousand miles away. My life has forever been changed because of our friendship.

ABOUT THE
AUTHORS

Cathy Parker and her husband, Carl, have raised four children, all at the ballfields. Cathy has experienced the extreme highs and lows of raising athletes and can relate to the toll athletics can have on the family. She founded the not-for-profits Athletes to Champions and Beyond the Ballfield to help athletes and their families deal with the realities of sports and use their influence for good.

David Thomas is the author/writer of more than a dozen books, including *New York Times* bestsellers *Wrestling for My Life*, with Shawn Michaels, and *Foxcatcher*—the story that inspired the Oscar-nominated film—with Mark Schultz. David serves as Pastor of Discipleship and Communication at Abundant Life Church in Grapevine, Texas. He previously worked for almost three decades in sports journalism. David and his wife, Sally, have two sports-playing children: Ashlin and Tyson.